The Man Who Sees Tomorrow in His Dreams

With Faith, So Can You

JOHN E. DESAUTELS

ISBN-13: 9781493518524
ISBN-10: 1493518526
Library of Congress Control Number: 2013919464
CreateSpace Independent Publishing Platform
North Charleston, South Carolina

Contents

Acknowledgments

I would like to express my sincere thanks to Martha Haley for providing many suggestions throughout the development process. I would also like to thank Mary Anne Ryan whose comments helped me reshape the manuscript to better focus on my story.

My sincere thanks go out to Claire Gardner, Archivist for The Edgar Cayce Foundation, who took the time to review my manuscript and check my references to the Edgar Cayce readings. In addition, I thank her for her suggestion for improving the subtitle of my book.

The team at CreateSpace made the process of moving my book to print a painless experience. From the support team to the design, editing and marketing copy, the response was timely and effective.

Most important of all, I would like to express my love and gratitude to my son whose encouragement and numerous questions over the years made this book possible.

Introduction

I think the single reason that my life evolved the way it has is that I've paid attention to something that others either did not notice or quickly dismissed as unimportant. From my earliest childhood (before I was five years old), I can remember recalling dreams. I am able to pinpoint the timeframe because my father died from a kidney disease when I was five. Before his death, sometimes I would walk in my sleep and awake in my parents' bed. I can still recall my mother consoling me after a particularly frightening nightmare. She said it was only a dream and that it didn't mean anything. There was a discussion between my parents about why I had so many dreams, and my mother expressed certainty that I would grow out of this behavior. I'm not sure my father believed I was having dreams; I think he viewed it more as my attempt to not sleep in my own bed.

I had two brothers, Robert, who was nearly two years older than I and was my constant companion, and Bill, who was twelve years older and had little impact on my early life, but who later became a surrogate father. Robert didn't understand my dreaming because he didn't think he dreamed. I often remembered my dreams from a very early age, and my brother and childhood friends did not appear to recall any. This simple fact lay dormant in my consciousness for many years, but would eventually become a key aspect of my life. I would notice increasingly an enhanced awareness of my physical and emotional state and events surrounding me—past and present, as well as the future. This book describes that evolution.

With expanded awareness from my dreams, individual issues and challenges were made clear to me, often in very graphic forms. New career opportunities were revealed, along with directions for change in order to realize my full potential. I also dreamed of broader issues that affected my employer, the economy, and the world at large. I found myself projected into airliners that crashed, and I saw homicides and suicides before they occurred. More than once a dream saved me from serious injury. After many years of study, I have found the following pattern: My dreams clearly foreshadow the next day's events, usually in the order in which they occur.

As with other aspects of life, the value of an enhanced or enlarged awareness is what each individual makes of it. The potential is available to enrich life with a sense of direction, providing insight that may help in navigating challenges that might otherwise hinder or overwhelm a person. My purpose in this book is to take the reader along a path that will assist in opening one's awareness to this potential. I describe a simple process for achieving that potential, which can be used by anyone willing to devote a small amount of time each day to meditation and the study of dreams.

Although it may have been easier for me to remember dreams than for most people, scientists have verified that everyone dreams. Most individuals can be trained to recall dreams, and the functions of their dreams are similar. In this respect we are all alike. There is nothing that I have done that anyone else can't do— and in some cases do even better.

There are several places in this book where I use terms other than God as synonymous with God. Sometimes I use what Cayce called the Universal Forces or my choice of the Eternal One. Others have used different terms, but the intent is clear from the context and from the capitalization of the word or words.

One

PROPHETIC DREAMS

My first prophetic dream after leaving school occurred in Dayton, Ohio, where I had taken a job as a systems analyst with a small high-tech company engaged in image analysis and research in photographic science. My job was challenging, but my boss seemed pleased with my progress, so I looked forward to the six-month review. It was standard practice to review a new hire's performance after the first six months on the job, but raises were rarely given. I did not expect a raise and thought a dream I had experienced quite odd. One night a few days before my review meeting with my boss, I had a dream in which I received a raise that was nearly 15 percent of my salary. I knew from comments by other employees that raises that large were not given unless someone was being promoted, and I wasn't about to be promoted.

When I met with my boss, I was shocked to learn that I would receive a raise that was the exact amount seen in the dream. He justified it by saying that after reviewing my starting salary, he felt it was on the low side, so he decided to give me a raise to bring my salary more in line with others' salaries.

MY DREAM GUIDANCE CAME IN MANY FORMS

My dreams provided feedback and guidance throughout my work years. I saw company reorganizations before they were announced, layoffs before they occurred, potential sources of conflict or people to avoid, people I should seek out for assistance, opportunities I should pursue, and a host of other things. Probably the single most important benefit from my dreams was my enlarged awareness of people and situations around me. This helped me defuse arguments and get the best from those who reported to me. It also made me aware when I was unknowingly offending someone in some way or just not getting a point across.

In my personal life, I was advised about how to improve my health, made aware of coming disasters, warned about dangerous people and situations, shown financial opportunities, and guided in ways to have a positive impact on friends and family.

In my later work years, I began to notice that more and more my dreams accurately reflected my next day's activities and challenges. I was living the day twice, once the night before and then the actual day.

As a young man with a son less than one year old and my wife ill, I found myself out of work in Florida due to cuts to a government-funded program I was working on. After working a few years in Ohio, I had moved from Ohio to Florida to enjoy warmer weather and improve job opportunities, which obviously didn't happen. I recall a powerful dream a few weeks before I was laid off that showed me losing my job, but the dream also indicated that everything would be OK. I was told that we would have enough money to get through the period, and that I would have a new purpose in life. The dream ended by showing me playing a tiny piano that I would later learn related to my teaching spiritual concepts I had recently encountered in an Edgar Cayce study group. In the dream, I remarked that I couldn't possibly do that. A person present as an advisor in the dream said that I would be able to and would not find it difficult.

I reviewed our finances and things looked bleak. And the job situation in Florida for high-tech was terrible due to government cuts in defense spending. I had few interviews and no job prospects. Then, unexpectedly, I got a call from my last boss in Ohio. He said he had heard I was out of work, and they had a new project for which he thought I was a good fit. With no other prospects, I flew to Dayton for an interview and later accepted the job.

DREAMS PREPARE THE WAY

Years later, when I retired and decided to move to Florida to be close to my son, who was living in the Tampa Bay area, I had several dreams about the relocation. After a visit to Florida, I considered several properties and made an offer on one. Then I had a dream with a warning that I was making the wrong choice. I reconsidered and withdrew my offer. While meditating, as opposed to dreaming, I received an answer that directed me to the right property. My decision to buy this property was confirmed as the right thing to do in a dream. This experience is further described in chapter 5.

During my several trips back and forth to get resettled, I also experienced another type of dream that I have come to find very comforting over the years. One trip was by air, and the night before my scheduled departure, I dreamed I was on a plane listening to an announcement from the pilot that we were going to experience a rough landing due to turbulence. I remember reflecting on the dream, and even mentioning to my son that I thought I was going to be in for a tough trip. Since I did not foresee a crash, I went ahead with the scheduled flight. True to my dream, the warning announcement came from the pilot prior to what was a very rough landing.

When I go on a trip, I always reflect on my dreams from the previous night for any signs that might alert me to danger or some unusual occurrence. During my lifetime, on at least two occasions, I have had dreams about plane crashes. On these occasions, I was with other passengers on a plane that suddenly plunged from the sky with a crash imminent. I experienced the terror and chaos in the plane as a real event. Within a few days after these dreams, a commercial airliner in some part of the world crashed, killing all passengers, so I pay close attention to dreams of this type.

My retirement years are good because I prepared properly for them. This was due in no small part to guidance from my dreams that helped me achieve the lifestyle I desired. Several years prior to my retirement, I began to focus on my finances to ensure that I could in fact retire at some point. During this period, I had some dreams concerning precious metals and their future value. These dreams were very specific. In one dream, I was shown a graph for the price of gold and its future behavior. In another dream, I was told that the place to invest at the time of the dream was in platinum. The dream advisor said that silver was the place to invest later on.

For the next several months, I watched as the price of platinum soared. During the rise in the price of platinum, I did extensive research on gold and silver. I became convinced that silver was undervalued and would have to rise over the long term. In addition to being a precious metal and in demand for coins and jewelry, it has many industrial applications. The demand for silver had exceeded the supply for several years, and the once-vast stockpiles of silver were gone. I did not wait for silver to move higher and bought it at about five dollars per ounce. I did not know how long "later on" was. Since my dream, the price of silver has reached a high of forty-eight dollars per ounce, and as of May 13, 2014, has fallen to below twenty. I sold some of my silver when I retired and made a nice profit.

Although I made money from silver based on dream guidance, I was not trying to see the future of silver prices through my dreams when this occurred. The dreams just happened as I was seeking good investments. I found that my dreams become confusing, fragmented, and of little value if I try to use them solely to seek material benefit, regardless of the justification.

CHANGING THE FUTURE

My book is about using the expanded capabilities of the mind to see the future that is being built and changing that future to reflect the soul's purpose. And when I say I see tomorrow, I mean I see my activities, the people I meet and with whom I interact, and how I think and feel. A few years ago, I planned to meet up on a Saturday with my son at his house before going to a boat parade. Earlier in the week we had agreed on a time, but as the time approached, he called and said he needed to move the time back a half hour. So I went to a café in an organic food store and drank coffee before driving to his house. I clearly remembered two dreams from the night before.

In the first dream, I was in some type of restaurant, and I was seated in a booth. A woman passed by, and our glances met. She smiled, and there seemed to be a special acknowledgment. Perhaps I reminded her of someone. She was a slender blonde and quite attractive. A moment later she was gone, but then in what seemed like short time she walked by again. In the second dream, I was in a house seated by a woman. Off to one side was my cat, Happy, who had died many years ago. Happy had a red ridge on his neck, and the woman said she had taken the collar off due to the irritation on his neck.

Now, while drinking my coffee in the café in the organic food store, a café I would not have been in if my son had not called to push back our meeting time, I encountered a woman who was an attractive, slender blonde. When our eyes met, there was an immediate acknowledgment. She smiled and then disappeared down an aisle. A little later, I saw her check out. After about five minutes, she came back and again passed by me as in the dream.

When I arrived at my son's house, my daughter-in-law (now ex-daughter-in-law) was doing something with one of the cats. I sat by her and looked at the cat who was now off to my left and noticed that his collar had been removed and his neck had a red ridge on it. She said that the cat had gotten some kind of irritation on his neck, so she removed the collar to help it heal. Prior to this visit, my brief talk with my son about changing the time was the only communication I had had with him in several days, and I had no knowledge of the situation with the cat.

These are simple examples, but they demonstrate how my tomorrow was lived in the unconscious the night before. An understanding of this was the basis for the changes I made, where change was possible, and enriched my view of life, death, and who and what I am. Of course, my dreams were not only about the future, but were problem solving, reflected conflict and emotional states, provided instruction and direction, and accomplished a host of other purposes that are explained in dream books and discussed in the chapter "My Dream Language."

When dreams are combined with intuition, I find that they form a powerful duo for accessing the subconscious in a safe, reliable way. As my own consciousness expanded over the years, I no longer felt alone or subject to the vagaries of an impersonal, indifferent world. I now had a degree of control over my life and could fashion the life I wanted in a way that was consistent with the best that is in me.

This chapter illustrated a few of the benefits of seeing the future through examples taken from my own life, and more examples will be provided in the following chapters. In the next chapter, I discuss how and why my serious work with dreams began. In the remainder of the book, I explore how seeing the future unfolded for me and lead the reader into the process I used, which can be adopted by anyone who wants to follow a similar path.

Two

Taking the Plunge

In Dayton, Ohio, my wife and I started an Edgar Cayce study group to work with the material in two small, red books called *A Search for God*. The material in these books had evolved from the readings given by Edgar Cayce for a group seeking greater spiritual awareness. And at this point in our lives, my wife and I were both seeking greater meaning. We had been introduced to a Cayce study group while in Florida, which is where my work with dreams started. The group provided an opportunity to hear different peoples' dreams and share common experiences. My interest in dreams was stronger than most of the others in the group, and I think I got more out of my dreams because I worked harder at it. Edgar Cayce said many things about dreams, but my focus turned to the following claim he made about prophetic content in our dreams.

EVERY SIGNIFICANT EVENT IN OUR LIVES IS FORESHADOWED IN A DREAM

This Cayce claim fascinated me and became a key driver in my life. I was determined to use myself as a test case to see if it was true. This was a critical time for me because this decision would set the course for the remainder of my life. I decided to examine all my dreams for both guidance in my personal life and evidence of Cayce's claim. Unfortunately, some people in the Cayce study groups in which I participated only focused on dreams that showed them in a good light and ignored the others as meaningless. I believe this was and is a major mistake; I found that the dreams that show our problem areas, where change is needed, are the ones that should be the focus.

I still remember the woman who only attended a few meetings, but in those few meetings managed to antagonize everyone. She was critical in her speech, and in her conversation about the people in her life, she revealed a strong tendency to verbally tear people apart. In her last visit with the study group, she described a dream in which people around her were being attacked by vicious animals. She didn't have a clue as to the meaning. I saw her in a mall several weeks later and asked her if she was going to return to the study group. She said she didn't think so, and that she believed her dreams really didn't mean anything after all.

THE IMPORTANCE OF RECORDING DREAMS

I first learned that I needed to record my dreams on a daily basis. Meanings are often found only when the dreams are examined over an extended period. To recall dreams was normally not a problem for me; in fact, most days I recalled so many dreams I found it difficult to record them all. On those few occasions when my dream recall was poor, I followed a simple procedure that I discuss in the chapter "My Dream Language."

The months went by and my dreams did not seem to foreshadow the coming events in my life, although at times there were striking exceptions. Back at my old job, I worked in a satellite building a short distance from the main building. One night I had a dream in which two tornadoes struck the company buildings. A small one struck the building I worked in, and a large one struck the main building. I knew enough about dreams to realize that it was not good news. I thought about my job and could not see any signs of problems for the company. However, within two weeks layoffs were announced due to the unexpected loss of some government contracts. The layoffs were minimal in the satellite building where I worked and quite substantial in the main building. My dream had prepared me for what was coming, and as a result I was able to get through it much better emotionally than many of my colleagues. I now had another example of a very clear precognitive dream, but it was the exception.

DREAM PATTERNS FOR ANSWERS

After I had recorded about three months' worth of dreams, I was somewhat frustrated by what I saw as a lack of progress. So one Sunday afternoon I began to review them for common elements. As I went through dream after dream, it became obvious that the same theme repeated in different guises. I also noticed some dreams showing my mailbox overflowing with uncollected mail. I began to try to interpret the common themes in the dreams. In numerous dreams, I was involved in various sports, scoring baskets or goals, but in my actual job, I was lacking confidence and did not feel successful. The Florida experience had been a serious blow to my self-esteem, and I didn't like my current job. In fact, I was miserable and felt trapped with no way out.

During that period, I also had a dream showing me as a slave on a slave ship. In the dream, a voice said it wouldn't be nearly as bad if I didn't struggle so much. I didn't fully understand the message at first, but I later realized it was telling me that I needed to go with the flow even if I wasn't yet in a fulfilling job.

These dreams gradually began to cause an awakening. It didn't happen overnight, but I slowly began to see that I could find other opportunities at work and did not have to be the victim of circumstances. I could be successful and score points if I let my natural abilities find expression. In these dreams, my subconscious was focusing on what was important to my overall health and well-being. With the exception of an occasional prophetic dream, dreams of the future had to await this more critical need. Now, once I really understood the dreams and integrated them into my conscious thought, that pattern of dreams stopped. The mail had been collected. The message had been received and understood.

I believe the importance of how my dreams evolved cannot be overstated because this evolution explains why some think dreams are rarely precognitive. Researchers who study dreams may well conclude that there is little evidence of precognition, and for the group chosen, that may be true. The dreams of the group may be dealing primarily with daily-unresolved issues, so evidence of precognition may be limited as it was in my case.

THE PRACTICE OF MEDITATION IS KEY

In addition, another factor here is very important. As part of the study group activity, we meditated as a group during each meeting. And regular daily meditation was recommended in the Cayce material. It did not take me or the other group members long to realize that the quality and clarity of our dreams were greatly enhanced by the regular daily meditation. Prophetic dreams seemed to increase in frequency. When someone once asked Cayce how he could improve his intuition, he recommended meditation. It has long been known by mystical branches of the world's religions that meditation can lead to heightened psychic awareness.

I had taken the plunge and the serious work had begun. I recorded dreams, looked for patterns in dreams, and attempted to start each day with meditation. And, of course, there was the attempt to put into practice what I learned, which proved to be very difficult at times for me and the other members of the study group. I found out how difficult very quickly when I had dreams that involved other individuals whose behavior I was encouraged to emulate. The dreams were very simple and to the point: *You should be more like...* These dreams were hard for me to accept because often I did not consider these individuals to be examples I should follow, and in a few cases, I disliked the person. It took a lot of soul searching for me to see the validity of the dream and be able to accept the message as helpful.

Over the years, I occasionally had this type of dream where the individual I was encouraged to emulate was a political figure. In one case, I was told I should be more like Lyndon Johnson in his ability to be friendly and take the time to stop and chat with people. At that time in my life, my dreams were trying to move me from an introverted lifestyle as a technical specialist to a more outgoing lifestyle, where I would be friendlier and take time to make small talk with people at work. On another occasion, much later, I was told to be more like Bobby Kennedy by asserting myself and standing up for my views.

Three

BUMPS AND SINKHOLES

MONITORING MY ENTHUSIASM

When I began to see the tremendous potential in my dreams, my enthusiasm became unbounded and expressed itself one day at work. I started discussing dreams with one of my coworkers and said that I thought we could see the future through our dreams. The individual was well educated, and I expected to have an interesting discussion with him. Instead, he lashed out at me and said he didn't want to talk about it. He said that he didn't care if it was true; he didn't want to know the future. He finished by saying in a loud voice, "I don't want to hear any more about it." At that moment his body language, with a display of violent arm movements, made it clear that the discussion had better end.

I learned that not all people are going to be receptive to my views, particularly when it relates to the metaphysical, so I became selective in my discussions. I found that people who were sincerely interested in subjects like dreams tended to be at the same events I chose to attend; I often found kindred souls at lectures, in a bookstore, or at a conference.

HEALTH BENEFITS

When I began serious work with dreams, I had not yet done some of the work on my health that would later take place, like regular exercise and a good diet. I felt lethargic while in Florida and still had health issues back in Ohio. My dreams began to provide help. During this early period back in Dayton, I would get dizzy at times and often lacked energy. In a dream, I was told that if I did not start exercising and stretching my spine, I would start passing out. I was given an exercise to do that helped greatly. In another dream, I was told that I needed a spinal adjustment, which I had performed by an osteopath.

I also had a prostate problem, and despite several trips to the doctor, I still experienced discomfort. One evening I was reflecting on my problem, and later that night I had the following dream. I was shown the front page of a newspaper. The pages began to turn, and I was shown car after car with comments on the suspension system for each. A voice said that my prostate problem was due to the suspension on the car I was driving. After this dream, I began to focus on my car's ride and realized it really was quite rough. I wasn't able to get rid of the car immediately, but later the prostate problem cleared up when I was able to buy another car with a better suspension system.

Another time, one morning I began to experience abdominal pains. I hoped it would get better as the day progressed, but it didn't. With trepidation, I decided I would have to visit the doctor the next day. That night I had a clear dream in which I was back in a supermarket where I worked while in high school and college. I was staring at the dairy case and noticed that the orange juice section was almost empty and the milk section was overflowing. The manager came by and with an ominous look told me I needed to take away some of the milk and add orange juice. The next morning I changed my diet to include orange juice for breakfast with no milk, and at the evening meal I would have one glass of milk. The problem quickly cleared up without a visit to the doctor.

I had many bumps along the way as I attempted to work with dreams and apply what I learned within and outside of the study group. I made mistakes in interpretation, and I was often too late in heeding warnings or taking advice. At times the progress seemed painfully slow, but then something would happen to reaffirm my faith in the path I had chosen. Sometimes, though, we experience not just bumps, but gaping sinkholes in the road of life. I discovered that when people seek to grow psychologically and spiritually, their surroundings and lives might change in a very pronounced way. And at times some of these changes certainly appear to be sinkholes that swallow up everything of familiarity and comfort in life. My sinkhole occurred about three years after my return to Ohio from Florida.

TERRIFYING AND PROPHETIC

The dream was very terrifying and caused me to be gripped by fear. In the dream, I was seated on a curb talking with my wife, Fran. We were sadly looking at a picture of our son, who had been killed in an auto accident. After some serious reflection, the fear subsided and I consoled myself with the thought that dreams are seldom literal. So what did it mean? It certainly wasn't a happy dream, even if it did not relate to my son. From my early studies and work with dreams, I learned that dreams are symbolic in nature, and they usually can be deciphered by thinking of associations for the symbols in the dream. In this case, our son represented something to which we gave birth that had just been killed off. The dream was prophetic, and I would later discover that it represented the death of our marriage. This did not happen overnight, but one singular event was the trigger for the dissolution of the marriage of two opposites.

For a few years after we first joined a study group, it was a joint activity. In Dayton, we could not find a suitable group, so we started our own. We continued in this way until it became clear that we were moving in the wrong direction during the meetings. Fran and I disagreed on the purpose of the group and the conduct of the meetings. We both began to feel that we could not express ourselves openly in the same meeting. I joined another group and began to move in a different direction than Fran.

However, the real turning point occurred when she received some money from her grandfather, who wanted his grandchildren to have it before he died. She decided to make a trip to Virginia Beach to attend a conference at the Association for Research and Enlightenment. Now, just prior to her leaving, I had a dream in which Fran was looking at a black-and-white TV picture, and a somewhat blurry image began to clear up and turned into a beautiful, focused color image.

When I met her at the airport upon her return, I knew something was very different. She was very distant and acted like someone in a trance. Gradually, I began to learn that something had happened to her while attending one of the classes. There was a guest speaker, not an ARE staff member, who said some things that triggered a radical shift in consciousness for her. The illumination caused her to see the world in a completely new and different way. This had been a moment of intense clarity for her. The impact of her experience gradually faded, but her insights only crystallized what we already knew, which was the incompatibility of our beliefs, goals, and overall basic approach to life. Because of this experience, she no longer saw herself in a role that could be made compatible with our marriage. After several more years of struggle, we filed for dissolution of the marriage.

The crumbling marriage took me into a long period of depression, and I found it difficult to meditate and work with my dreams. My lowest point was reached one evening when I sat in a chair numb from the reality that my marriage could not be saved. I actually started crying, which was a rare thing for me to do. I had grown up without a father, and now my son would not have a full-time father. Later, while asleep, I had a simple dream experience that was jolting. In it, I saw the vastness of the universe, and out of the vastness a booming voice said, *"Why are you crying? Don't you know you are immortal?"*

SICK CHILDREN

Fran and I were both searching, but for probably different reasons. Eventually our search led us in different directions, but there were times when we shared a common cause. Early in our marriage, Fran had discovered that a hospital for forgotten children was seeking volunteers. This hospital housed children who were so severely disabled that they could not function in society. Some were in a near-vegetative state and barely moved. A few had deformities like an enlarged head that was too big to be held up, resulting from a condition called hydrocephalus. A boy named Tommy, a hydrocephalic, spent his life upside down and moved around in a crib by grabbing the bars with his fingers and toes and pulling himself. His head was enormous and much too heavy for him to lift. Some thought he was violent; actually, I think he just wanted physical contact. He loved to grab someone's hand and squeeze it, and I can still recall his shrieks of delight.

Another child I remember was a little girl named Kristy. She had spina bifida and was completely rigid; she looked like someone who had just tensed up, but in her case there was never a release. Kristy moved little, but did manage a big smile. She was one of my favorites, and I would spend time holding her little hand. One night I had a dream in which I saw Kristy in this dark, depressing house. She was sick and appeared to be very distraught. On my next visit to the hospital, I discovered that Kristy had been very ill earlier in the week, and the staff had been quite concerned about her. They said she had a very high temperature and was in a bad way, but she had recovered by my visit.

Our volunteer work was more than sitting with the children. We changed beds and diapers, and cleaned up vomit. In short, we acted as practical nurses. It was a job I will never forget, and certainly made me aware of the sad afflictions some must endure as they pass through their lives. Whenever my life seemed dark and hopeless, I thought about these children and realized that I was still fortunate indeed.

Four

BEGINNING LIFE ANEW

THE END OF THE OLD

The shattering of my world did not just involve the dissolution of my marriage. I had been very active in a church, teaching a class in the adult education program, and I considered the study group activity a key part of my spiritual development. Both of these would end as well. The church I attended was not particularly supportive during my trials, and I felt a rapidly diminishing rapport with its members.

The final blow came one day when I attended a talk conducted by a visiting minister who was sent to the different congregations by the synod to enlighten and inspire the church members. During a question-and-answer period, I asked a question and during the discussion stated that I thought we could reach the divine by turning within through meditation. He groaned and said, "You're one of those." There was a sudden silence; no one came to my defense, and he ignored me and moved on. After that episode,

I realized I no longer belonged there and never went back. I was done with organized religion.

I had enjoyed teaching the classes on dreams. However, I gradually began to realize that the attendees, although enthusiastic at first, didn't really want to see themselves as they are or make any substantial changes in their lives. Most had a comfortable lifestyle with a good job, and they really didn't want to make fundamental changes in their lives. For them dreams were curiosities, not something someone should incorporate into daily life. They believed they were fulfilling their obligation to God through their church attendance and worship, and their concept of heaven was as a place to go after death as their reward for a decent life.

The study group activities ended because the group dissolved when the couple hosting the group moved to another state. I did not look for another group. I was struggling to understand why things turned out the way they did when I had the best of intentions. All the study and work with dreams failed to save my marriage. And I now felt somewhat like I had several years earlier; I was without purpose and direction in life. My job had improved, and I had greater satisfaction at work, but the answers to life's meaning and purpose seemed far away.

HELP FROM DREAMS

I began the long road back. This road certainly had its twists and turns, and there were numerous challenges along the way. However, my dreams never stopped providing advice and guidance, even when I ignored them or headed in the wrong direction, and a few times was seriously off-track. They always tried to move me back onto the right path and bring my life into balance. The psychic and prophetic content continued, and some of it is described in subsequent chapters. At times I deviated far from where I should have been, and without my dreams I might have had a much less fortunate life.

THE SOCIAL SCENE FOR SINGLES

I began to focus on my job and adjusting to having my son with me on every other weekend. I was no longer with the small high-tech company. The company was sold to a larger corporation, and I was now working in a sister division doing systems analysis. Since I was now single again, I decided to explore the Dayton area to meet people and find events of interest. I was not looking for a wife, or even a girlfriend. I had various interests that included music and literature, and I just wanted to meet interesting people. So I began to explore the singles scene, which included bars and social groups.

A few early episodes convinced me that I had little tolerance for alcohol and should limit my alcohol consumption to an occasional glass of wine, so much of the time I had a Coke when in a bar. I picked a popular Dayton social group and attended some of its functions. I also attended some of the activities held by Parents Without Partners. At first, I was enthusiastic about meeting people and making some new connections.

I soon realized that there was little glamour to the bar scene, whether it was a dance club or local pub. I was not alone in my reentry into the single life, and I quickly discovered that many of the men and women I met had deep emotional scars. The women I tried to engage in conversation were extremely defensive, and it was obvious that the building of any level of trust would require a long-term effort. In most cases, I didn't want to spend months trying to prove that I was not like their ex-husband or ex-boyfriend.

The scene at the social functions I attended was different, but not much of an improvement. The people were better educated and had more money, but I found most of them to be superficial. I met a few men who had been divorced for much longer than I had and were quite familiar with the singles scene. They appeared to be reasonably intelligent, but I found their view of women to be a bit shocking. They told me that all of the women were screwed up and I should not take any of them seriously. Their view was that you never tell them the truth. Everybody just seemed to be out for himself with no real belief in much of anything.

During the first few years after my divorce, I did meet a few women who I thought were nice human beings. I just didn't have much in common with them, so I did not date them. I do recall two women whom I did want to date. One was well educated, and we had some common interests. However, she had issues, and my dreams indicated that it would be best to avoid her in a dating situation. The other one was not as well educated, and one night a dream made it very clear that we really had little in common. I did not seem destined to find someone to even date.

One night in a dream, a voice said that I would only have one wife in this life. However, I thought I ought to be able to find someone I could date socially. A number of times on business trips or at trade shows I would meet someone with whom I had an immediate rapport, but we lived in different cities, worked for different companies, and were moving in different directions. My boss at work, who had made me a manager, said that his wife had a friend who was recently divorced, and he offered to fix me up with her. At first I declined, but after several pleas, I agreed to go on a double date with my boss and his wife. My date was actually quite attractive, and I did take her out again. However, there just wasn't any real connection.

My boss was also the subject of a very interesting dream. One weekend I dreamed that I saw him with a red, disfigured face. I couldn't make much sense out of the dream until I arrived at work Monday morning. My boss walked out of his office displaying a very red and blotchy face. I was shocked and asked him what happened. He said over the weekend the family visited an area by some woods, and he had become exposed to a poisonous plant. My subconscious again collected relevant data that it fed to me in the dream.

DEATH AND A PROPHETIC DREAM

During this period, I would sometimes meet a friend of mine in a club that was at a halfway point and a convenient drive for both of us. In this club, I talked to a girl who took a liking to me. It was only casual conversation; she just wanted someone to listen to her problems. She had a hard life, and at the time seemed to be having problems with a man she knew. During our last conversation, she talked some about him and told me that he had been a student at a local college, but had taken some time off from school. The conversation was not particularly memorable and gave no indication that I can recall of what was about to occur.

Several weeks later, I had the following dream. In the dream, a girl was lying on a dirt road with her head crushed in. I didn't think much more about the dream until a few days later, when I turned on the radio on my way to work. The news announcer said that a young woman's body had been found on a dirt road. I instantly knew that it was the girl from the club. Later, the manager of the club confirmed my shocking psychic awareness. He said he identified the body for the police, and it appeared that someone had run over her head multiple times, crushing her skull. After an investigation, the police arrested a man and charged him with vehicular homicide. I don't know if he was ever convicted of the crime.

A PROPHETIC WARNING

During this same period, when I was exploring all aspects of the single life, I would sometimes drive several miles to a restaurant-bar known for good sandwiches. I used to sit at the bar and eat my lunch. It was not very busy, and I would talk to a young, female bartender who served me. She was very friendly, as bartenders often are, and I learned that there was an employee she had previously dated who was having a hard time accepting their breakup. One evening I had the following dream. I saw a man in the dream in the setting of that bar, and a voice said, *"He has a gun and is dangerous."* That was enough for me to stay away.

I did not see this girl again for a long time, but one night I was downtown in the locale of some popular restaurants when I encountered her with friends. I asked her how things were going, and she started crying. I hadn't said anything to upset her, so I was flabbergasted. After a minute or so, one of her friends said that her ex-boyfriend had gone to her house and gotten into an argument with her mother. The man shot and killed her mother and was sent to prison. This girl was fearful that he would get out and kill her too, so she was preparing to move out of Dayton.

I think I was somewhat fascinated by all aspects of life. Perhaps this is the writer in me. I had begun to write short stories, even before the marriage dissolution, and eventually had enough for a book. Often, when I went out in the evening, I was just interested in watching the people and observing the events unfolding around me. As I stated earlier, I normally would have a Coke if I was in a bar, and I never did any drugs, legal or illegal, other than the alcohol mentioned earlier. I was more an observer of life, rather than a participant. During this period, or later, I never shared an apartment, condominium, or house with anyone else. Other than when my son was visiting, I lived alone.

THE WORLD OF PSYCHICS

Another activity I engaged in was the exploration of the world of psychics. I was receiving information through my dreams that could be considered examples of clairvoyance and prophecy, so I was interested in how my insights compared with those of professional psychics. I began to attend psychic fairs, which are held regularly in or near large cities. I also attended lectures given by people who were purported to have some unusual paranormal ability. I have had readings from highly regarded psychics, as well as from lesser-known ones. In general, I have to say that most of them had limited psychic ability and had no impact on my life. Compared to my dreams, their readings were insignificant.

A few did demonstrate what I thought was an extraordinary ability, but most of what they related I already knew from other sources. Psychics often employ psychometry in their readings, which is the ability to sense things from vibrations associated with objects. They might hold a person's watch or ring in order to tune into the person.

Most of the psychics I interviewed claimed varying degrees of clairvoyance and clairaudience for paranormal abilities. A few relied more on a gut reaction, which is called clairsentience. The ones who claimed clairvoyance would see images in response to questions. They would in turn attempt to interpret what those images meant, which in some cases I found to be a mistake because the symbolism might only be relevant to the person asking the question. In a few cases I recall, the psychics initially only conveyed their interpretation, rather than what they saw, and missed the mark.

The psychics who claimed clairaudience normally would not hear a voice that was coming from an external source, but became aware of thoughts or an inner voice as if someone was speaking to them in their mind. In some cases, they claimed awareness of a presence that they identified as a guardian angel or spirit guide, who provided the answers.

The psychics who relied more on clairsentience said they could sense the feelings and mood of people and situations they were asked about.

A RARE TALENT

I did witness a man from England give a demonstration that was truly remarkable. People in the audience each placed an object on a table. A large number of people were present, so the table was filled with jewelry and other objects of all types. I placed a ballpoint pen on the table, but due to the large collection of objects, I did not think mine would be chosen. After selecting and reading from several objects, he came to my pen. He was very specific in what he saw; the details were extraordinary. He profiled what I had been doing at home the previous few weeks, which was not a normal activity and included a habit I had developed of which I was not even aware. However, I felt that he was a bit quirky and high-strung, and he did not strike me as a balanced individual.

DREAMS ARE THE BETTER WAY

After several years of exploration, I concluded that some professional psychics do have considerable psychic ability, but for most it is more limited than they believe and could not begin to compare to my own dreams. Also, most psychics, particularly those who employ psychometry, seem to be primarily reading the past. They could not tell me what will happen in the future. I cannot think of any significant predictions concerning the future made by them that have come true for me.

For many of the psychics who claim they are guided by an angel or heavenly host, I think their subconscious has created the entity. I believe this is also true of many of the deeply religious who claim to be in daily touch with God. The messages they attribute to God are most likely coming from an aspect of their own consciousness, not a universal source. I say this because the ones I have met who claim this guidance often seem to have personal psychological issues, and I sometimes find their messages to be the opposite of what a loving God would send.

The greatest of the religious mystics and saints have warned against the tendency to accept blindly voice messages as being from God. Studies have shown that in an unhealthy mind part of the consciousness can split off and declare itself to be anything it wants, even the Almighty. Some argue that the message must be from an angel, spirit guide, or God because things are revealed that they did not consciously know. I don't think this proves anything about the source being external; it only demonstrates the natural psychic power of the subconscious mind that I witnessed repeatedly through meditation and my dreams.

In the early '80s, I began work on a dream book, and in 1983 I sent it to several publishers, which included one recommended in a dream. This publisher expressed an interest, and the reviewing editor asked for some changes. I worked feverishly for three months to complete the changes. Upon finishing my revisions, I sent her the new manuscript, and one day I heard some good news and some bad news. The good news was that she loved the changes and was recommending that they purchase my manuscript. The bad news was that she was retiring in a few weeks. She turned my manuscript over to another editor, who succeeded in losing it. After several communications, it became clear that he was not interested in the subject and did not want to pursue publication.

After this, I put the book aside for many years and later rewrote it. I believe the new book is superior to the old, but it is not yet published. However, much of the personal material in it is contained in this book.

My dreams have commented on all my writing efforts. In one dream, I was actually given grades for my dream book and my book of short stories. I found this feedback helpful. It provided another perspective for my conscious efforts and caused me to reevaluate my works. The grades did not correspond exactly to my conscious opinion, but did provide strong encouragement for me to continue my efforts.

One message from my dreams was very clear. If I wanted to be successful with my literary works, I needed to be persistent in my efforts to be published. My dreams had little sympathy for me if I gave up. In fact, I was told in a dream that I should not have given up on my attempt to have my short stories published, which was a brief effort I made many years ago. Therefore, my next project will be to correct this past mistake.

Five

MEDITATION AND INTUITION

BACK TO THE BASICS

After my adjustment to the single life, I decided to refocus and get back to the basics, which included meditation each day and working with my dreams. I felt like my life had taken a wrong turn in some key areas, and I was determined that it would not continue to happen. I was not yet completely satisfied with my career, and my marriage had dissolved. My conscious deductive reasoning alone had not worked very well in several aspects of my life, so I needed a new approach. I needed a way to determine if I was on the right path and to avoid the pitfalls that result from unenlightened decisions. I believed that the practice of meditation and application of guidance from my dreams provided the answer, and I renewed my efforts in these areas.

MEDITATION AS THE STARTING POINT

Meditation is really the starting point for the spiritual path that I embarked upon in Florida, but I wanted to provide some background before discussing this topic. I believe it will make more sense at this point after the discussion of my study group activities, and it will naturally integrate with what was discussed in the previous chapters. I digress here a bit to provide the reader with the background and understanding I had at the time as I first began to meditate.

MEDITATION CONTRASTED WITH PRAYER

While prayer is asking the Eternal One for help, which is an active, directed process, meditation is defined as listening so the Eternal One may be experienced directly. I found there are many techniques for entering into meditation, but in the Cayce approach that I followed, meditation is consciously forming the highest ideal or concept of a higher power one can imagine, holding that ideal so that it may be realized or expressed through you, and then listening.

Although many Americans would immediately think of Eastern religions and yoga when meditation is mentioned, the Christian church is rich in its own tradition. Christian mystics meditated and wrote about their experiences. *The Cloud of Unknowing* is a classic fourteenth-century work on Christian mysticism that describes the form and practice of contemplative prayer, which forms the basis for modern-day Christian meditation. Regardless of the approach, the objective is to still the conscious mind, penetrate the cloud of unknowing, and move into the source of being itself.

PURPOSE OF MEDITATION

There is no universal agreement on how to achieve a still mind, so different methods have arisen for that purpose. Some use prayer, and others use breathing techniques or mantras to evoke the proper mood for entering into the silence.

The traditional view seems to be that one must meditate for years before there is any hope of eventual enlightenment, but sometimes enlightenment can occur after only a brief period. I had a friend in college who had a true transcendental experience after only several weeks of practicing meditation. The time required to achieve results is considered dependent upon the desire and readiness of the individual, not the calendar.

Meditation is a key part of the Cayce material found in the *Search for God* books. He stated that everyone should spend time each day in meditation, preferably in the morning before the day starts. When asked how long one should meditate, his response was that the length of time isn't what is important, but what one does with it the rest of the day. The idea is that one listens for some sense of attunement to the Universal Forces, and then is guided by it throughout the day. In the Cayce approach, one should not spend hours in meditation for its own sake, but should be doing something positive in the world.

For many of the great Eastern spiritual masters, meditation is the process of seeing or comprehending the wholeness of life with a quiet, attentive mind, and not something to be practiced at a set time each day. Some Eastern masters claim they are in a continuous state of meditation. There are also Christian mystics who spend long periods in meditation, but the practice does not appear to be as prevalent as it is among certain sects in Buddhism and other Eastern religions.

MEDITATION AND THE CHAKRAS

The classic treatise on Eastern meditation is The *Secret of the Golden Flower*, which is a Chinese meditation text. It describes the process of opening what are called the "chakras" or energy centers—also referred to as spiritual centers. The opening of these centers through meditation results in a natural experience of heightened powers and eventual enlightenment. As a result of opening what are called the higher centers, one naturally becomes more psychic, which often takes the form of clairvoyance or clairaudience.

Edgar Cayce also discussed the "kudalini" or life force, as it passes through the chakras. When asked how one could become more psychic, his answer was first to challenge the person's purpose. Then, with the right purpose, he recommended meditation. The Christian mystics who regularly practiced meditation were also well aware of the psychic development that is a natural offshoot of meditation. Cayce advised people not to seek to become psychic, but to develop their intuition instead. By this he meant one should listen and be guided by the still, small voice within, the Spirit of Truth or Universal Forces. Cayce and others have said that we can all develop our psychic ability. It is part of what we are. However, there are strong warnings that the use of psychic ability for selfish purposes such as just to control others or accumulate wealth will lead to one's undoing.

Even before joining a study group, I believed that material wealth was not the key to happiness, although certain basics are necessary. With that realization, I sought my soul's purpose. And for this I turned to meditation and a study of my dreams. I found my dreams greatly enriched and easier to remember if I meditated regularly. My dream content is best when I meditate every day, as I stated in an earlier chapter discussing study group activity.

I do not believe the method of meditation is nearly as important as intent and desire. However, a few basics can be helpful in leading a person into meditation. Breathing techniques can be used to calm the body, and closing the eyes has the effect of shifting our brain waves from beta, the normal conscious state, to alpha, more characteristic of deep relaxation and light sleep. Mantras can also help calm the mind and lead one into the silence.

GUIDANCE THROUGH MEDITATION

I discovered that there are several ways to receive guidance when I meditated. It may be a sudden thought, an inner voice, a knowing, or I may see an image. If I was praying for help with a problem, I meditated and listened for an answer. If I did not receive the answer in meditation, I often found it in my dreams or through a flash of insight during the day. These are all ways that the Spirit of Truth provided an answer. The Bible is certainly filled with stories of prophets and famous dreams that changed the course of events. And I did not think such prophetic dreams ended with the New Testament.

In the spring and summer of 2001, the words *twin towers* came into my consciousness while meditating. This occurred on at least three separate occasions. At the time, I couldn't make much sense out of it. I didn't think about the World Trade Center. My thought was that it somehow related to two professional basketball players who were referred to as the twin towers. It wasn't until the events of 9/11 that I understood the meaning. I had repeatedly seen through my dreams that our minds are connected on deeper levels and are constantly processing and filtering information.

Usually, I received information that related directly to me or those close to me, such as family members and friends. Our mind is said to attune or resonate to certain patterns. Some compare it to tuning a radio to pick up what a particular station is broadcasting. A person has to tune to the right frequency; the information broadcast by stations at different frequencies is not received. Otherwise, we would be so inundated that our conscious minds would not be able to handle the load. However, sometimes when an event as horrific as the attacks on the Twin Towers is about to occur, the information breaks through and many people become aware of it.

Several years ago, I was searching for a condominium or villa in an area near St. Petersburg, Florida. I turned within for guidance because I was having little success in finding a place that met my criteria. While meditating, an image of a choir popped into my mind, along with the words *Mormon Tabernacle Choir*. This is a good example because I often received answers through meditation symbolically, like in my dreams, as a play upon words. I have become quite proficient in decoding the meaning of symbols, and with a little effort, I related it to one of the areas I was considering. The development is called Bardmoor, and with a parsing of the word, we have bard, which can mean a singer of songs, and moor, which is very close to Mormon. I also had some dreams related to my house search, which confirmed this area as where I should buy. I purchased a villa here, which is well suited to my needs.

GROUP MEDITATION

There is strength in numbers. The combined presence of many seems to be greater than the sum of the individual efforts. In group prayer or meditation, individual progress can be accelerated. I have felt or sensed the additional energy during study group meditations. Some have suggested that the power is proportional to the square of the number involved rather than the number. I don't know if there is any formula, but at times I have felt the awesome power of group meditation. The coming together or meeting of people of like interest and purpose for meditation can happen anywhere; it doesn't have to be in a church or public building. Some groups hold their meetings in a member's house, which can create a more relaxed atmosphere. The group can also provide a support network that can benefit all its members.

Meditation is the subject of numerous books and at first was a bit confusing for me as a beginner. I soon found, however, that in its essence, it is simple, and I don't think it should be made into a complicated process. It is the process of letting go of all the concerns of the conscious mind. My progress was defined by how successful I was in moving past the constant mind chatter into a realm that is beyond the ego, one that contains the truth of who and what I am. It was dependent on how well I could release the ego and penetrate the cloud of unknowing to reach my true self. Sometimes I could accomplish it in five minutes, and at other times, I was still experiencing my mind chatter after a half hour.

In the next chapter, I will explore in more detail the process of how I received guidance from intuition or the inner mind. As I mentioned earlier, this can take many forms, but may relate to which sense a person favors or relies upon the most. I, like many other individuals, am more attuned to one particular sense perception, which may have influenced how my intuition developed.

Six

SHARPENING INTUITION

MY VIEW OF INTUITION

Historically, intuition has been associated more with women than with men. It is often described as a right-brain-versus-left-brain phenomenon, with women seen as more involved with their emotions and intuition, and men with logic and reasoning. Of course, both right and left halves of the brain need to work together to provide a full set of human abilities and experience. Although this characterization of the difference between men and women may not be correct as a general statement, I think it is still a view shared by many.

The psychic field in particular seems to find credence more readily among women than men despite the fact that many of the best-known psychics or *intuitives* like Nostradamus and Edgar Cayce were men. I have attended lectures and workshops on metaphysical topics where those present were 80 to 90 percent women. Maybe this is because women can easily relate to premonitions they have concerning their children. My mother was not schooled in the metaphysical, and with her Roman Catholic background, she would not have accepted very many metaphysical beliefs. However, she did believe strongly in hunches and premonitions. I think this is one of the reasons that I have been able to accept intuition as a real ability. I don't think men are limited by their gender; they are only limited by their biases. I think intuition is available to all.

WAYS I RECEIVED GUIDANCE

My use of my intuition soon began to yield positive results. In my case, I found myself able to receive concrete answers to problems through inner visions or clairvoyance. Through my investigation of psychics and study of the Edgar Cayce readings, I learned that one's intuition could provide insights and guidance in many different ways. The method may depend on a person's psychological makeup and how a person relates to others and events. I thought it important for me to identify my sensing tendencies as a person because they might give me clues about how I could best receive intuitive flashes or insight. I found that my strength is more along the visual lines, but I still sometimes hear an inner voice or have a strong feeling about a person or situation.

EXAMPLES OF GUIDANCE

When I attempt to tune in and receive guidance, I first watch for inner images in response. The image often conveys the answer or help I am seeking in a very clear and economical way. There are exceptions, though, such as what occurred a few years ago when I was considering the purchase a car. While driving home from a restaurant, I had a strong feeling I should pull into a car dealership a short distance ahead on the right. It was Sunday and the dealership was closed, but I was able to examine the used-car selection. I found just the car I had been seeking, and I still drive it today.

An earlier time, over fifteen years ago, I was in the market for a used compact SUV. After some searching, I found an SUV that met most of my criteria. In meditation, I asked if this was the right choice. I immediately saw an image of the car and a person who repeated *"for you"* several times. I drove this SUV for five years maintenance-free except for routine service like an oil change.

There is another sense that can be experienced as well. It is one of an inner knowing, which is what happened when I knew the dead girl lying on the dirt road was the same one I had talked to just weeks earlier. I didn't see an image or hear an inner voice; I just knew that something was true. Some call this claircognizance, and this sense may be common because I often hear people say they know something to be true but don't know how they know.

During one of my most stressful times at work in the early '90s, I was facing total disaster on a large special project. Our customer was going to use our equipment in a new application, and a team from their customer was to arrive the next day for a test demonstration before final approval. The system did not work, despite a Herculean effort by a project leader and a programmer. I remember slumping in a chair at home, wondering what my next job would be after I was fired. I started to meditate, to turn within, and sought guidance. An inner voice told me that the project leader would get the problem fixed in time. It didn't seem possible, but just hours before the group arrived at the site, the system was up and running. And our customer was awarded the contract.

MY INTUITION DEVELOPED WITH USE

My intuition grew in strength with use and became as normal as my other senses. I started with small things that did not endanger me in any way. As I began to listen to the messages and develop my intuition, I found that it became easier to access it and most of the time was able to separate real intuition from wishful thinking. Instead of an occasional, unpredictable psychic flash, I am able to receive help and guidance in a reliable and timely way. At this point, I believe I have succeeded in merging my conscious and subconscious abilities into a more integrated and aware consciousness.

THE FINE LINE BETWEEN INSANITY AND INTUITION

Unfortunately, there are well-known examples of people who have committed the most heinous crimes under the direction of a voice, often believed by the person to be the voice of God. The psychotic serial killer sometimes blames his murders on direction from God or some human authority figure. There are other examples where the harm is more restricted to the individual who hears the voices. The book and movie *A Beautiful Mind* tells the story of John Forbes Nash, Jr., who won a Nobel Prize in economics based on his mathematical contributions. After the age of thirty, he began to show signs of mental illness, and his life became a struggle with schizophrenia and paranoid delusions. John saw imaginary people with whom he conversed about threats to himself and the political system of the United States. John Forbes Nash, Jr. eventually leaned to deal with his demons and turn his attention back to more rational scientific thinking, but throughout his life, there has been a fine line between his intuitive mathematical genius and psychosis.

So I wondered how to know if what I see or hear is real, dependable intuition or the psychic manifestation of a psychological or physiological disease. I think this is where balance comes into play. There is considerable discussion of mediums or psychic channelers in the literature. This is not a new phenomenon; it was widely practiced in the 1800s. Some authors such as Hudson in *The Law of Psychic Phenomena* do not paint a very attractive picture of them and warn people to avoid such practices. According to Hudson, many mediums are highly temperamental and seem to have trouble balancing their own lives with that of the trance.

Although also very temperamental, Edgar Cayce was different because he did not channel entities like mediums and psychic channelers do, and he repeatedly warned against relying upon anything except the highest power. He advised people to stay away from Ouija boards and automatic writing because a person has no way to know what he is attracting. He said it isn't because they don't work; it is because they work in an unpredictable, and sometimes detrimental, way.

I concluded that there might be gifted psychics and channelers who provide access to an entity or presence from an alternate reality, but I see this as unnecessary when a person has the ability to get answers in a safe and balanced way through meditation and dreams.

MY INTUITION DEVELOPED THE SAFE WAY

By developing my intuition through meditation and working with dreams, my psychic ability grew naturally, as I was ready for it. And my dreams provided continuous feedback on how I was doing, in order to keep my conscious self from extreme and unhealthy behavior.

By contrast, I think drugs, unless administered under the supervision of a professional psychotherapist, can be dangerous as an artificial means to experience nirvana. The conscious mind is flooded with images and impressions that it is often unable to integrate, resulting in a personality that can't come to grips with daily existence. The only answer becomes one of escape because there is no conscious structure to support the array of feelings and visions found in the subconscious that seem so foreign to normal conscious life.

On the other hand, studies have shown that dreams, as products of the subconscious, are always seeking balance and the well-being of the dreamer. I was constantly given insights to help me grow, but ones that didn't overwhelm my conscious mind to the point that it could no longer function in a meaningful way.

I FOUND NO SHORTCUT TO SELF-AWARENESS

I don't think there is any shortcut to a self-aware mind. Psychologists say that issues, often deep and traumatic, from the past must be seen in the clear light of day, resolved, and then dismissed so focus can be turned to the next challenge. Resolution is critical because suppressed fears and emotions find a way to spill out, often contaminating other aspects of life. My attitudes and values were formed early in life, like everyone else, so there was considerable baggage that was carried throughout my life.

A study of dreams and the practice of meditation helped me sharpen my intuition and awareness so I didn't add to that baggage and could begin to release what was no longer needed or fruitful. I have seen many friends and acquaintances get divorced over the years, and some jumped back into a marriage that was no better, sometimes far worse, than the one they left. The application of a developed intuition could certainly have saved them the resulting grief. I couldn't change the life I lived prior to my work with meditation and dreams, but I could change my life going forward and make better choices and decisions. When, in or after meditation, I found myself concerned about the message I received, I considered this: If the message and feeling from meditation was not loving and life-enhancing for everyone, then I needed to examine myself and my purpose and question my source of guidance.

READING MINDS

As my intuition developed, I noticed that on rare occasions I would appear to be tuning in to someone's thoughts. One such occasion occurred in a restaurant near work where I often had lunch. I became friendly with a waitress who was working toward a degree at a local university, and we talked about a variety of topics. One day, when I sat down, she looked at me and I heard her voice as an inner voice that said, *"Why doesn't he ask me out?"* Now, I wouldn't have been surprised if this came through a dream. I frequently had dreams in which I saw and heard what people thought of me or thought I should do, which some may regard as an invasion of privacy.

At this point, I will say that I never try to read another person's mind. However, I have repeatedly found through my dreams that we are all linked on a subconscious level, and there really is no thing such as privacy, whether we like it or not. I will have more to say about this in later chapters as I continue to examine prophetic dreams and their effect on my life. In the case of the waitress, I don't think it was wishful thinking because I had no desire to date her, and I did not ask her out.

Seven

My Dream Language

INTERPRETING MY DREAMS

Up to this point, dreams have been a key part of my story, but I have not provided many details on how I worked with dreams. In this chapter, I delve more deeply into the process of interpreting dreams. I investigate further my dream language and give a sampling of what I learned in working with dreams for over forty years. What I found is based on actual day-to-day analysis and application, as well as on material from the Edgar Cayce readings and numerous studies. Without question, there are a great many books on dreams, and after I started working with my own dreams, I read some of the popular books on the market at that time. However, my dreams are primarily about me, the dreamer, and they are generated by my own mind, so I believed I was the person best qualified to decipher them.

I found that books containing lists of dream symbols along with their common meanings were of limited value. The meanings given suggested to me some things to consider, but I learned that the symbols in my dreams are unique to me and have special meaning because of the events in my life that only I can know. I have heard lectures on dream interpretation given by people who—I later discovered—really did not work with dreams on a regular basis in their own lives. This always surprised me because I found that dreams had to become incorporated into my daily life before I could really understand them.

Dreams have been widely studied by neurophysiologists and psychologists. In this book, I am focusing on the psychological aspects of my dreams and not the physiological processes associated with my dreaming. However, I did some research on the activity of the brain during dreaming to understand how dreams relate to the various stages of sleep. And what I found explained why my strongest dreams were normally the last ones and the easiest to remember. I include a summary here, which clarifies what I discovered with my own dream cycles.

THE STAGES OF SLEEP

Scientists have measured the electrical activity of the brain during both waking states and sleep states. An instrument called an electroencephalogram records the electrical activity associated with the firing of neurons in the brain through electrodes placed on the scalp. The signals generated are analyzed in terms of their frequency content or cycles per second. The highest-frequency waves are called beta waves, and they occur during our waking state when we are very agitated or focusing hard on some intellectual activity, such as solving a problem. The brain waves in the next range are called alpha waves and are associated with relaxation or daydreaming. The theta waves come next and are characteristic of light sleep. Finally, we have the delta waves, the lowest-frequency ones, which are characteristic of deep sleep. When we daydream or are very relaxed, we can easily slide from beta into alpha. As we drift into sleep, the brain waves also slow down, and we pass through various stages of sleep. At each stage, the physiological processes of the body slow until we are in the deep sleep characterized by delta brain waves. It should be noted that when I say characterized by I am referring to the dominant frequencies; this does not mean that other frequencies are not present to some degree.

Normally, after about ninety minutes, we begin to have dreams with associated rapid eye movement (REM). At one time, it was thought that all dreams occurred during this REM period of sleep, but it was later discovered that people dream during non-REM sleep as well. During REM sleep, when the strongest dreams seem to occur, the brain activity increases to higher frequencies. So during REM dreams the person passes from deep sleep, characterized by delta waves, to an alpha or even beta state in terms of dominant brain frequencies. The REM dreams increase in length during the night with the longest one being the last, and they have been found to make up about 20 percent of our total sleep at night.

As a side note, I can say with certainty that we sometimes dream much sooner than ninety minutes after falling asleep, even if the dreams are not part of REM sleep. I frequently take naps and can awaken after a half hour or less with the clear memory of a dream.

Some believe that during delta sleep our unconscious passes into what might be called the universal mind and is able to tap into a collective unconscious. It would certainly be interesting to know the composition of the brain-wave patterns of Edgar Cayce when he was giving a trance reading. However, his life predates the research with such measurement devices.

REMEMBERING MY DREAMS

After deciding to explore dreams, a person's first concern is often about how to remember dreams. That everyone does dream has been scientifically confirmed by awakening people during REM sleep, even if they normally don't remember them. Although remembering dreams was not usually a problem for me, sometimes I had periods without dream recall, so I decided I would adopt the following procedure to ensure that I was remembering and recording as many dreams as possible.

I purchased a notebook and kept it by my bed, along with a pen. Some people use a recorder instead. Before falling asleep, and as I drifted off, I gave myself suggestions to remember my dreams. I realized that it might not work the first few nights, but I was prepared to be persistent. When I first awoke from a dream, whether in the morning or middle of the night, I quickly learned not to immediately get up. I found that if I did not first concentrate on the dream to make sure I had it firmly remembered I would sometimes lose it before I got the pen and notebook. Dreams can be fleeting, and the simple act of getting out of bed, or even moving, can result in the loss of a dream.

Once I started to recall dreams, I didn't always want to sit there in the middle of the night and record the entirety of it, so I had to make sure I recorded enough of the dream to retain it.

The next morning I would fill in the details. After several years of working with dreams, this became unnecessary. My focusing on the dream to commit it to memory was sufficient.

MY RECORDING OF DREAMS WAS ESSENTIAL

I found that recording dreams was extremely important, especially in working through the issues in my life. This is because my dreams occurred in patterns, and if I couldn't decipher an individual dream, when I perused several weeks of similar dreams the meaning often became obvious. In addition, many dreams with a similar message, like my dreams showing me scoring points in various sports, demonstrated the importance of the message, and I couldn't progress beyond them until I understood and acted upon the information.

I discovered that interpreting a single dream that is part of a pattern is like my walking into the middle of a movie and, after a minute or two, trying to understand the entire plot. I might be lucky and hit the right moment, but more than likely, I spend the rest of the movie trying to figure everything out.

I had some nights with no dream recall, and the number of dreams I recalled varied from night to night. After I developed proficiency with dream recall, I was able to recall at least two dreams per night and as many as five. I think one time I recalled seven from a single night, but five is normally the maximum number I can remember. My sleep hours were usually regular and my dream recall was good, but occasionally on the weekend, I would have a late night and my dream recall suffered. This was also the case if my sleep was erratic due to nasal congestion or concerns over some problem.

MY DREAMS WERE NORMALLY SYMBOLIC

After I recorded a week or two of dreams, I started the process of understanding them. This is where the real work began. I found that my dreams were rarely literal, with a few exceptions that I discuss later. My dreams were symbolic, and the symbols often contained an amazing economy, conveying meaning on multiple levels. I started out by looking for a practical meaning as it related to my daily life.

Dreams can be esoteric and may even relate to past lives, but the majority seems to deal with the mundane. I decided to correlate my dreams with my life. I would note at the end of the day the major events that had occurred during the day. These might include a sudden encounter with someone not seen in a long time, an argument with a coworker, a moment of real bonding with someone, an interesting or strange telephone call, a problem with my car, or anything else that stood out to characterize the day. I believed that as I studied my dream patterns across many days, I would be able to discover the interesting and strong correlations with my daily life. If the precognitive content was there, I should be able to see previews of the next day's key events. I was gradually able to do this, but as I pointed out earlier, I first had to resolve issues in my life before the content fully emerged. So I recorded my dreams in the morning before they slipped away, and I recorded the day's main events at the end of the day. I did not write or need long paragraphs for the day's events, just enough of a note to know what was involved.

The events that occurred in my dreams at first seemed bizarre and often nonsensical (they could be brought about by drugs or reactions to what one eats, but this is not the majority of dreams for most people). This is why in relation to dreams one often hears, "They don't mean anything. They are just nonsense." Far from being nonsense, the subconscious mind was using words, images, and events from my life to convey important messages in a way that best represented the message.

As an example, I have had dreams in which I was naked or I saw someone else as naked. Upon awakening, I thought about the Freudian implications and wondered what it was saying about my sexual thoughts and desires. I soon realized that the person I saw, whether me or someone else, was not going to become naked. I found that the person naked in the dream had become exposed in some way, sometimes emotionally. The dream, making use of metaphor, saw me or the other person as naked or exposed. If it was another person, normally the person in the dream was not the actual person that would become exposed; the person in the dream was like that person in some way and reminded me of that person. Once I understood that this was how my dreams worked, I had a much easier time interpreting them.

A common dream is for a person to see or feel his front teeth crumble, break off, or just fall out. I have had several of them over the years, and I once had a waitress in a restaurant relate this type of event as a recent dream. She was quite upset because she had expensive crowns on her upper front teeth and was panicked by the thought that they might break off. I asked her to think about what had happened in her life the day before and day after she had the dream. She thought for a moment and then appeared a bit embarrassed. She remembered that the day before the dream she had been in a violent argument with her boyfriend and had said some mean, hurtful things to him. I think a likely interpretation of the dream is that her teeth symbolized the words, and her ugly appearance afterward symbolized how the words made her appear to her more spiritually evolved self.

On a few occasions, I dreamed that someone attacked me with a knife or other sharp instrument. I awakened in a sweat and immediately gave thanks that it was only a dream. Only a dream, but what did it mean? In the case of most of those dreams, I recently had been attacked verbally in a way that made me feel as if I had been sliced up, and verbally and emotionally, I had been. In one of those cases, the dream event was a preview of what was to come the next day.

Of course, not all dreams are violent or disturbing; some were peaceful and took me to incredibly beautiful places. Often the environment was a university campus where I attended lectures or met with a wise person who provided advice and counsel that related to current problems in my life. Sometimes I experienced astral or soul travel. In these dreams, I enjoyed ease of movement that was controlled by my thoughts, and traveling above a building or to a distant location was as easy as seeing myself there. The sense of freedom was exhilarating and gave me a sense of life separate from my physical body.

UNIVERSAL AND PERSONAL SYMBOLS

From my reading, I learned that some symbols in dreams are rooted in mythology and religion and are more universal. Carl Jung classified them as archetypes that contain elements of man's past that are deeply imprinted in the psyche and are common to all humans. Examples of these are the animus, anima, and the wise old man or old woman. These symbols seem to share common meanings across everyone's dreams. However, even these symbols can contain an aspect that is unique to the individual dreamer. So I always have to ask what the symbol means to me.

As I said earlier, books suggested some possible meanings, but only I could determine the full meaning and significance of a symbol. This is because emotional content differs from person to person. A friend and I may have dreams that involve cars. For both of us the car represents transportation, the power to move from one distant location to another, but one of us may have a love affair with cars, while to the other the car is only transportation. The emotional content of the symbol is very different and can affect the interpretation of the dreams. (I found that my car dreams often related to the physical body, and the condition of the car in the dream reflected the condition of my body. An example of this is a rusty car that suggested a need for exercise in one of my dreams.)

My dreams used exaggeration to emphasize a point or message. Perhaps this jolt to my mind helped my consciousness remember the dream so that the message was not lost. An example of this is my dream of a car that was falling apart, which was shown in the dream as something that appeared to be headed to the junkyard. This did not mean I was going to die, but the dream accurately depicted how I felt at that moment.

To summarize my remarks about symbolism, my dreams used simile, metaphor, allegory, and exaggeration to convey messages to my conscious mind. In some instances, they were literal. The best example of this is a dream that contains a critical message, such as a warning. In the dream, a telephone rings, I pick up the receiver, and a voice delivers a message. The subconscious considers the message so important that it delivers it as a verbal, unambiguous message.

I have had a few dreams of this type during my life, such as a telephone call concerning my son who was having a problem with a bully in preschool, and I can attest to the fact that the messages were literal and involved critical situations of which I was consciously unaware. Sometimes a voice just delivers a message without the telephone. My dreams warning that something bad is going to happen if I don't heed the warning are usually of this type.

I have also had dreams, normally involving family members, in which I encounter a person and learn about some issue or problem the person is facing. Whenever I had a dream of this type, I later learned that the dream was an accurate depiction of the person's personal struggles. Some of the background in the dreams, such as the place where we meet or other details, may not be literal, but the emotional encounter with the person is a literal depiction of what the person was experiencing at that point in time.

Sometimes I went several days without much, if any, dream recall. At first, I was quite concerned, but I then realized that important problem areas in my life would be seen in the dream patterns over many weeks, so I would not miss important messages. I found it easier to remember the dreams that occurred closer to my normal hour of awakening. They are both the strongest and the longest dreams, so they were more likely to be in my memory upon awakening. Sometimes my last dream of the night seems to go on forever. I can awaken with the memory of the dream, doze back off, and be right back in the dream where I left off.

CLASSIFYING MY DREAMS

Now I am going to separate a further discussion of my dreams into the following classifications: physical ones dealing with health, mental ones dealing with work and my economic and social life, spiritual ones dealing with my religious life, precognitive dreams or dreams of the future, dreams of death and dying, past life dreams, and lucid dreams. Obviously, there are other ways to classify dreams, and if this were a tutorial on dream interpretation, I might take a different approach. However, as a condensed version this will serve my purpose in further discussing my dream language.

HEALTH DREAMS

I have already said that the car or automobile often served as a representation for my physical body in a dream. In addition to the previous examples, this worked the following way. I had a dream in which my car had flat tires. At the time of the dream, I was feeling flat, without energy.

Another time, I dreamed that I was driving a new car that was a smooth-running, high-performance model. I had made changes to my diet and was exercising regularly, and I was starting to feel energetic and that I was firing on all cylinders in my life.

A dream about a car with a damaged wheel meant a problem with the corresponding limb.

A few times, I have dreamed that my car battery was dead. Usually when a dream of this kind occurred, I felt a loss of energy to get started in my daily routine. However, on one occasion

I discovered that I had a dead battery in my car. Dreams of this type normally reflected my physical condition; they did not tell me what to do to change it. They were reminders of my condition and that corrective action was needed to address the problem that showed up as a defect in the car. When I review my dreams, as I stated earlier, I always look for an obvious, practical answer first.

Dreams about my health occurred in numerous other ways as well. A good example is one described earlier concerning a problem with my prostate that I experienced as a young man. The dream's commentary on suspension systems for different models of cars made clear the cause of the problem and gave me some potential solutions. The dairy-case dream about milk and orange juice is another example of how my health issues were addressed in dreams.

In still another dream (precognitive), I watched a single drop of blood as it fell to a surface. A voice said, *"In ninety days."* Suddenly, the scene changed and I was sitting in a chair in what appeared to be some type of doctor's or surgical office. A nurse stood beside me and a doctor performed some type of procedure. Then the dream ended.

As ninety days approached, I became a bit apprehensive about what might occur. At what was exactly ninety days, I got out of bed in the morning to find the vision in my left eye quite blurred, as if some huge particles had found their way into my eye while I slept. I looked into the mirror, but could not see anything. I already had some floaters, but this was quite different. I made an appointment with my ophthalmologist, who said what I was seeing was dried blood, usually the result of a tear in the retina. He couldn't see a tear, but quickly got me an appointment with a retina specialist, and within two hours I was seated in a chair with a nurse beside me as the doctor sealed a small tear in the retina with a laser.

Another time in a dream, I saw all sorts of numbers from a blood test, and a voice said the salt content of my blood was too high. I dreamed about my overall health in many different ways, but the car often served as a quick reflection of my overall condition and energy level.

DREAMS ABOUT WORK, FAMILY, AND SOCIAL LIFE

Once I got past my health issues, improved my diet, and increased the amount of daily exercise, I found that the bulk of my dreams dealt with my work, family, and social life. Struggles and opportunities at work, as well as in my social life, were reflected in my dreams. I quickly discovered a very important point: There is no such thing as private thought or actions. I was taught by the many books I read that in the metaphysical world thoughts have a real existence, and others who are able to tune into them can "see" them. It is one thing to read this, and it is quite another to actually experience it. Initially, I think I was horrified by this. I wanted to draw a firm boundary between others and myself and to have a private space, where some things were sacred that no one else could ever know. However, this is not the case.

Through meditation and my dreams, I discovered that we are all connected at a subconscious level, so there really is no such boundary. If I tried to hide something from someone, that person may very well dream about it. When I had my first encounter with someone who had experienced a dream about me that revealed something I wanted to remain secret, I was quite shocked and upset. However, apparently there are no absolute secrets. In the greater mind, all appears to be known, right down to the most miniscule detail.

Edgar Cayce demonstrated this repeatedly through his readings, and I found that a good psychic could sometimes pick up what I considered my most secret thoughts. Scientists performing studies at dream laboratories have confirmed the existence of thought transference and the linkage of subconscious minds. This appears to be the way the real world operates, whether I like it or not. Every action I take and every thought I have is recorded, and everything I do affects everyone and everything in the universe. It is like dropping a pebble in a lake or stream that sends out a tiny ripple that causes every part of the water to be affected in some way. This has also been referred to as the *butterfly effect,* where, hypothetically, a butterfly flapping its wings causes a storm thousands of miles away.

Dreams about my working and social life were common and provided continuous feedback on how I was doing with my job and interactions with others, both at work and socially. If I started down a negative path, I would immediately see the warnings in my dreams. Sometimes I would see myself in a dream with improper clothing, or tears and rips in what I wore. Alternatively, my clothes might be soiled. Other times, I lost my luggage or took a wrong turn off a highway.

If I was moving in a positive direction, I received feedback in the form of dreams that showed my efforts in a positive light, often through the presence of beautiful settings with vivid colors, uplifting music, and overall harmony. I might be dressed in a new blue suit or have just received a thousand dollars. Dreams reflected back my attitudes about what I did, how I lived, and what I thought. I saw my thoughts and attitudes about other people and other peoples' thoughts about me as well.

I sometimes had dreams about insects. If my house was being overrun by insects such as ants, in my job or personal life I was most likely irritated by numerous small problems or annoyances, symbolized by the insects. Insects like wasps might indicate the problems have a sting to them. If I encountered larger problems or threats, I might dream that a vicious animal was about to attack me. Again, these dreams showed the state of my mind at the time of the dream. I knew what I needed to do to change the picture. I had to change my attitude and response to these problems. They were simply reminders of how I was being affected by the situation.

I found that dreams are a powerful source of help in solving problems. The subconscious has more resources than the conscious mind, along with a seemingly perfect memory and deductive capability. For maximum benefit, I proceeded in the following way. I began by working at solving the problem with my conscious reasoning mind. If research was required, I did the homework. After I had exhausted my conscious resources, I asked for help from a dream before falling asleep. I tried to be specific; if I had arrived at a conclusion or answer, I asked for confirmation. If I couldn't find a solution, I asked for an answer that was in harmony with what was best for everyone involved.

Similar help can also be obtained directly through prayer and meditation, especially when faced with a yes/no situation. Cayce suggested the following approach (Edgar Cayce Reading 2072-14). Reach an answer through your conscious efforts. Take the question into meditation, and listen for an answer. If you have reached the right conclusion, the answers should agree. I have successfully used both approaches for solving a variety of problems.

Whereas dreams of the state of my health often involved a car or other motor vehicle, dreams about the state of my daily life often involved my house or apartment. The rooms related to different aspects of my life. A kitchen in a dream often related to my diet; when my diet improved, I saw an improvement in the appearance of the kitchen in my dreams. Prior to making major changes in my diet, I frequently ate burgers from one of the fast-food chains. One night I had a dream showing me that I should put this type of food into the garbage disposal.

The living room related to how I lived my life. A sunny living room showed me that my daily life was positive and cheerful. A dark, dismal living room indicated that some light needed to come into my life.

The family room related to my entire family as a unit and provided some clues on how the family as a whole was faring.

The bedroom sometimes related to sex, and other times it simply reflected my sleeping patterns. The interpretation depended on its role in my life at the time of the dream, and these meanings appear to be common. Some symbols are often considered phallic symbols such as a gun or anything that is long and tubular in structure. As a phallic symbol, the firing of a gun has an obvious meaning.

The bathroom in my dreams sometimes related to purification of some kind. In one dream, a plugged toilet symbolized a need for me to purge myself of certain thoughts and attitudes. In another dream, it seemed to relate to a physical health issue.

I found that upper levels in a building related to my conscious mind or spirit. A lower level like a basement related to my subconscious. If I had a dream about a beautiful house I had moved into or built, this was a positive affirmation about my daily life. However, when I found myself in a building with a leaking roof or walls that were in poor condition or collapsing, an analysis of my life at that time revealed that there were problems and that certain areas of my life needed to be addressed right away. The extent of the damage was an indication of the severity of the problem; small leaks were small problems, and torrents of water pouring through the roof or walls indicated major problems.

Dreams about my economic or financial condition were often broad in scope, particularly since my employer sometimes had difficulties, and the entire country has witnessed catastrophic economic problems. The tornado dream I had during my early years of employment in Dayton is an example of dream guidance in relation to the health of the company where I was employed. During the stock market crash of 2008–2009, I was completely out of the stock market, having been prepared well in advance by my dreams. As described earlier, during the period from approximately 2000 to 2005, my dreams showed me that precious metals would be a good place to invest.

I had some very specific dreams concerning both gold and silver. When I first started having the dreams, both gold and silver were depressed and considered very poor places to put one's money. Although volatile, as of May 13, 2014, gold is over $1,200 per ounce and reached a high of $1,900; many experts think it will eventually go to $2,000.

When I watch a segment on the business news, I often hear how unexpected the 2008 collapse was and how no one could possibly have foreseen what happened to the housing and banking systems. I, as well as others using meditation and dreams for guidance, did not find this to be the case. My dreams clearly showed that there were dangers in the economy and markets prior to the collapse in housing.

Gordon Michael Scallion, considered by some to be a modern-day Nostradamus, had a newsletter called *Intuitive Flash* (discontinued in 2012 and replaced with an e-mail service), in which he gave his predictions for the year in the January issue. Sometimes his predictions concerned events he saw developing several years into the future. I have followed his predictions for many years. He accurately foresaw the collapse of housing and banking in 2008, well in advance of reported events. And the sources for these predictions were none other than meditation and dreams.

My dreams have showed me that things do not just happen; I am not the helpless victim of unseen events that pop out of nowhere. Before my work with meditation and dreams, I was not listening, at least not in the right way. My work with meditation and dreams was not about how to get rich and have a life of luxury. Others who have gone before me in following this path have warned that if I try to use them solely to this end, I would end up greatly disappointed.

I have found that my dream content is best when I am trying to be of service to someone else. This does not mean that I ignored my guidance concerning my job and personal finances. These are all part of my daily life, and I needed certain things to provide for my family and enjoy all that life has to offer. I found that good fortune is the result of how I live, and I strive for balance in what I do.

I used dreams to help me optimize my performance in my vocation, and they helped move me to better opportunities when my current job was not satisfying or was stifling in some way. The first few years of my dream work helped me change my career and find a much more satisfying way to earn a living. It did not happen overnight; I first had to understand the patterns in my dreams and the limits I imposed on myself. Then I could begin to make changes that led me in a new direction. One of these changes was going back to school to take graduate courses in business to prepare myself for a move into management. When I was ready the opportunities came, and I no longer had the same dreams because I had resolved the issues.

One such opportunity was provided when my company selected me to participate in a weeklong course on situation analysis and problem solving. I performed well, and the instructor encouraged me to go into management. Another came when I was presented with the choice to stay in engineering or move to a new support group that was part of marketing. I moved to the new group and later became manager of the group.

My dreams go through cycles. I will see a theme building up, and then after the understanding and resolution of issues occurs, there is a new theme. Sometimes I feel like I have been shredded by a barrage of my shortcomings, and about the time I think I can't take anymore, I find a building process that encourages and advises, taking me to the next level. I constantly remind myself that the shortcomings are there even if I choose to ignore them, and that they will continue to negatively affect the quality of my life.

My social life was also strongly reflected in my dreams. Relationships were examined, encouragement was made, and warnings, when appropriate, were given. Just think of how much grief could be avoided if people tuned to their subconscious for guidance in their relationships. If I have heard it once, I have heard this cry from women a hundred times, "Why do I keep picking such losers for boyfriends?" I think anyone can get off the treadmill as I did, but I first had to know how to make a good choice.

Meditation and dreams helped me, but I had to be honest with myself and be open to receiving the guidance. There were times when I wanted to do what my conscious mind and desires dictated, regardless of what my dreams or intuition told me, but I soon realized that there was no point in looking to them for guidance if I ignored it. At times, I felt like the woman in one of the study groups in which I participated, who jokingly said she prayed, "God, help me improve my life and be a better person, but don't touch my eating and smoking." I discovered that what I learned about relationships with other people also applied to groups and organizations. I began to tune into my subconscious to pick up the overall flow of certain groups and their leaders, to sense whether the direction of the groups was compatible with my own.

I found revelations about the social structure of my family in dreams to be particularly important. My relationships with my wife and son were clearly revealed in dreams, not just my hopes or desires. In these dreams, I often met or conversed with someone who served the role of an advisor, and this advisor would sometimes give advice by stating things in a very clear, literal way. During the period when my marriage was disintegrating, there were numerous dreams of this type. They did not assign blame, but focused instead on pointing out things my conscious mind did not fully understand. This helped me deal with what at times were very challenging situations.

Comments or actions that have slipped by my conscious awareness were not missed or forgotten by the subconscious. This does not mean that I could or should use dreams to spy on a family member. With regular meditation and the right purpose, my dreams provided information that I needed to know in relationship to my health and the health of the family, and not what I might like to know that really didn't concern me.

Once I was seeking information through my dreams about a family member. That night I had a dream in which I was attempting to open a book. A man present, who seemed to be an advisor, said I would not be allowed to open that book. It was several years later before I understood why. If I had seen what was going to occur in the future, I would not have been able to deal with it at that particular time of my life and would probably have made a wrong turn. So my dreams did not just give me carte blanche for a look into the future; there was an important monitoring function performed by my subconscious.

SPIRITUAL DREAMS

I had dreams that related specifically to my spiritual development. In my early work with study groups, I asked myself the following: Are my life, thoughts, and actions in accord with my soul's purpose? Cayce said that dreams are a result of the soul taking stock of what one has done during the day. We have heard about the near death experience (NDE), where one sees his whole life flash before his eyes. Some have described the period right after death as a review of what one has done with his life. My dreams provide sort of a minireview that occurs nightly.

In spiritual dreams, I often found bright colors along with symbols such as water, the cross, or a wise old person. A grandparent or someone who represents teaching to me, such as a former teacher or advisor, was sometimes present. In my early years of dream work, my advisor from graduate school served the role of a spiritual advisor in some of my strongest spiritual dreams.

Police or judges were often present to symbolize spiritual law. In the dream, if I broke the law and was arrested or appeared before a judge, I was undoubtedly doing something in my personal life that violated spiritual law.

I saw spiritual progress symbolized by swimming smoothly and effortlessly in a body of water. I sometimes dreamed that I was listening to beautiful music, or found myself in a setting such as a green field surrounded by lush vegetation and an assortment of beautiful flowers, again symbolizing a rich and fruitful spiritual life.

Cayce and other metaphysical teachers consider colors very important. Colors such as purple or lavender are considered spiritual colors, along with some shades of blue. These colors are also associated with the higher chakras or spiritual centers. The lower spiritual centers are represented by the colors red, orange, yellow, and green. Red is often associated with life force, sex, or anger in a dream. The color yellow can symbolize sunshine or cowardice, and green can symbolize healing or jealousy. Orange is associated with energy and health. Of course, colors may take on a different meaning in dreams, depending on a person's associations and feelings about certain colors. The same may be said of numbers.

There are some meanings ascribed to numbers by Cayce and others, but the actual meaning is always dependent upon the person's feelings and associations. Common meanings for some of the numbers are as follows. The number one is representative of the Universal; three, of the three Christian aspects of the Universal (Father, Son, and Holy Spirit); four, of the lower four spiritual centers; five, of change; seven, of the spiritual (seven chakras or spiritual centers); and nine, of completion. The receipt of a spiritual gift was often represented in my dreams by my getting one dollar—or some multiple like one thousand.

When I first started working with dreams, I found that the color and condition of the clothes in a dream told me how I was doing. Also, since shoes are what we stand on or what provide support for the body, the condition of my shoes in a dream often symbolized the state of my spiritual foundation. I always check both the color and condition. In my first few years of working with dreams, I had numerous dreams with spiritually relevant clothing colors and involving coins of highly symbolic amounts.

PRECOGNITIVE DREAMS

In my pursuit of evidence for precognitive dreams, I was well aware that dreams that relate to the future (precognitive dreams) have been a source for scientific study for some time. They also provided the basis for themes invoked by the entertainment industry, and I think my interest was definitely increased by movies and TV shows that invoked this concept. Scientists have conducted numerous experiments in sleep laboratories to either prove or disprove the hypothesis that dreams can foretell the future.

The subject of precognitive dreams is not new; these dreams have been part of important stories from the Bible such as that in Genesis of Joseph and his brothers. However, the real confirmation for me of precognition in dreams came from the evidence in my own dreams. One of my early experiences with precognition in a dream occurred at my first job out of school, before I even started to study dreams. I saw the financial results of my review before the actual review occurred. Other examples that have been given include my dream about the tornadoes hitting my place of employment, dreams concerning the precious metals market and its future behavior, and the dream about the tear in the retina of my eye.

Taken in isolation, one could write these off as coincidences. However, the flood of dreams with similar precognitive content over the years goes far beyond coincidence. My dream about my boss with the red, inflamed face is much harder to attribute to coincidence. And my dream about the tear in the retina in my left eye was incredibly accurate, right down to timing and the procedure used to correct the problem. These are significant dream examples, but in addition to these, there are literally thousands of daily occurrences, like the examples of my encountering a woman when having coffee in a café, and finding one of my son's cats with a red ridge on his neck when I reached his house.

DREAMS OF DEATH AND DYING

A type of dream that many people find disturbing concerns death and dying. When someone has a dream about his own death or the death of a loved one, it is usually so frightening that the person fights to forget the dream and suppress any further dreams. When I first had dreams about someone close to me dying, like my son in one dream and my mother in another, I was terrified. I think this is understandable, but I now find it is unnecessary. My dreams of death and dying rarely meant that an actual physical death was about to occur. Let's look at a few of my dream examples.

I once dreamed that my mother was in a coffin being lowered into the ground. At that point in my life, I had given up all desserts and foods heavy in sugar, and had made other improvements to my diet, as well. My mother earned her living as a cook, and during my years growing up, she always had various pies, cakes, and cookies around. She liked sweets, and I was raised on them. I think her being lowered into the ground symbolized the burying of my consumption of desserts, which she represented. In fact, my mother did not die until many years later.

In another dream, which I recounted earlier, I learned that my son had died. Again, what was dying was not my actual child, but the relationship or marriage between my spouse and me. The child was symbolic of what we created or gave birth to in our relationship that was now dying, and which was depicted in my dream by the view of the photograph of my son, who had been killed in an automobile accident. What does a dream that I am dying mean? I may simply be dying to the old to be resurrected to the new. Of course, if I am endangering my health in some way, the dream may be saying that I am killing myself.

So how do dreams depict actual physical death? This can be indicated in a variety of ways. A clock with stopped hands is one way. I once dreamed about someone and saw a clock with the hands moving a short distance and then stopping. That person lived only a short time after my dream. Before my mother passed over, she had been ill, and her organs were shutting down from old age. When the time came, a few nights before I dreamed I spoke to her as she was leaving a small room. She said she was so glad to not have those restrictions anymore.

DREAMS OF PAST LIVES

One of the most controversial areas relating to dreams is reincarnation or past lives. Here by reincarnation I am referring to a person having lived many times on the earth as different personalities through one soul that incarnates. I am not including the Eastern doctrine of transmigration, where souls inhabit other forms of life. The concept of reincarnation, which is a belief in some Eastern religions, is also fundamental to New Age doctrines. There are some Christian sects as well who believe in reincarnation, but conservative Christians are vehemently opposed to it and challenge anyone to find concrete proof in the Bible. I am not going to take up this controversy, but I will say that I do accept reincarnation and that I have experienced certain dreams that I believe relate to past lives.

There is a belief that dreams about past lives are in costumes and surroundings found at that period in time. In addition, the belief is that past-life dreams occur to help clarify one's current life and the issues and challenges one faces. The dreams of mine that I consider past-life dreams meet both the criteria of being period dreams and having some important relation to my current life. I was not some great person in my dreams, and I can't say that I was engaged in any unusual activity. However, I faced certain challenges in those dreams that have influenced my current life. In two of the dreams, I even experienced my death and knew exactly what was unresolved when I passed out of each life. I think I have benefited from my reincarnation dreams, but reincarnation is not something I worry about or concern myself with each day. I try to live appropriately in the *now*, and I believe if I do that the rest will take care of itself.

There are individuals, though, who find much more comfort in a belief in reincarnation. Many years ago, when I was participating in an Edgar Cayce study group, one of the attendees at the meetings had been confined to a wheelchair his entire life. He was a man in his sixties and said he had spent most of his life in bitterness over his condition. He said he used to cry out, "Why me, God?" He found an answer through the doctrine of reincarnation, which changed his entire life. He became content and always looked for the positive in life. For him, reincarnation was the answer.

LUCID DREAMS

Lucid dreams, or dreams in which the dreamer is conscious that he is dreaming, became of great interest after the publication of *Lucid Dreaming* by Dr. Stephen Laberge in 1985. In a lucid dream, the dreamer participates in the dream and to some extent controls the course of the dream while being aware of dreaming. Lucid dreams are thought to have benefits for the dreamer by allowing the dreamer to work through issues in a setting where physical harm is not a threat.

Personally, I think there is some risk associated with lucid dreams. I have sometimes been conscious of dreaming while in a dream, but I have not pursued this area. My belief is that lucid dreams can become an escape from reality rather leading to beneficial results. I benefited from my dreams by accessing an aspect of my mind that was more aware and able to see my broader good. If I was creating dreams from my conscious mind, I don't see how that could benefit me in the same way. I can see a therapeutic value if a person is afraid to face certain potentially dangerous situations in real life but is able to meet and resolve them in the dream without the fear of physical harm.

This concludes this chapter on my dream language, but I will still have more to say about my dreams in later chapters. This description of my dream language is by no means comprehensive and only includes some of the more common examples of dream types and symbols. I have talked about different types of dreams, including dreams of the future, but I haven't yet addressed the question of how or why I think precognitive dreams are possible. This will be discussed in chapter 12.

Eight

CHANGE THROUGH DREAMS

MY NEED FOR CHANGE

True change is difficult to make, which many discover when they try to get rid of a habit like smoking, which was once my nemesis. Basic changes to the diet are just as difficult to make, if not more so. Although I was not overweight when I started working with dreams, my dietary habits were detrimental to my health. I ate too many pastries and foods high in saturated fats. My high metabolism probably spared me from becoming overweight.

After I began a study of Edgar Cayce and started working with my dreams, I realized that I really needed to change my dietary habits. Although I didn't yet have a weight problem, I didn't feel well. I lacked energy, frequently had colds, and usually contracted the flu during the winter months. Like earlier with smoking, at first I thought I could just reduce the amount of the *bad* items. So I tried to restrict my diet to an occasional pastry and cut down on the pizza and burgers. This worked for a while, but I soon was back with my old habits.

I think many people struggle in the same way. Whether it is food, alcohol, cigarettes, drugs, or something else, addictions are prevalent and seem to be growing. We now see video game and social networking obsessions.

MY DREAMS HELPED ME CHANGE

Did I find change difficult because I didn't want to change, or because I didn't know how? I think the answer is probably a combination of the two reasons. And the application of what I learned from dreams helped me with both, whether the issue was diet or some other behavior I seemed unable to correct. My dreams helped me improve my diet and overall health. I was urged to give up certain foods and add others, increase my exercise, and change my mental outlook. Several examples of my health dreams were given in the previous chapters. The barrage of dreams dealing with lack of confidence discussed in chapter 2 helped me change my job opportunities and guided me to more satisfying work.

MY DREAMS PROVIDED THE MOTIVATION

In the case of diet, my dreams often showed me the raw truth of what I was doing to my health through my dietary habits. Sometimes the dream just commented on my behavior. One night I was playing bridge, and during the course of the evening, I ate far too many potato chips with onion dip and drank much more wine than was normal for me. That evening I had a dream in which I entertained Babe Ruth, who was known for his excessive eating and drinking. I think the meaning of the dream was clear. Any time I abused my body through excessive eating, I was shown what I was doing in a very clear, unambiguous dream.

My dreams often showed conditions in an exaggerated way for effect, and if ignored the results might be all too true. I had already read or heard numerous accounts of what had happened to other people with similar problems. This may have temporarily given me reason for reflection, but it didn't cause me to change my behavior. However, when I saw my own individual future in graphic terms in my dreams, it caused more than reflection and helped jolt me into the reality of what I was doing to myself. Now, when I got the message from a single dream or a pattern of dreams and really intended to change, I received positive assurances and suggestions for change. The feedback mechanism of my dreams was great, and as I made changes, it soon became clear from my dreams if the new direction was a good one. After I made major changes to my diet, I dreamed that I was driving a new, high-performance sports car.

First, I had to take action, even if it was only a small one. My dreams did not just give me a list of things to do each day, although in the case of diet I was shown what foods to give up and which ones to add. I was creating my life from moment to moment, and I needed to exercise free will by making decisions and taking action. If my action was not a good one and was inconsistent with my higher self, I received the appropriate feedback. And when my decision and new actions were positive, I saw supportive feedback in the dream; for example, in the case of diet it came in the form of a beautiful new kitchen or a sleek new car.

MY SUCCESS WITH DREAM WORK
REQUIRED HONESTY

I did not always like the picture I received through my dreams, and at times I was angry and attempted to justify my beliefs or positions. When I was shown people whom I should emulate in some way, I didn't like it at all. This was a critical time; at this point, many people decide that dreams are unimportant and give up. During my years of working with dreams, there were several times when I thought about giving up. Each time, I had to reassert my desire to see the truth and reaffirm my willingness to change and move beyond the initial reaction, which was to flee from dreams and try something else. Then something always happened to confirm the value of dream work and this approach to life.

In this chapter, I selected diet and health as an example of one of my areas of change through dreams because it was an issue for me, and is a broader issue in this country today, causing untold misery for countless people. Obviously, I could have chosen something else like rudeness, which often manifests as the habit of constantly interrupting people during conversation or shows up in various ways among drivers on the highway.

I knew a lovely woman in the church I attended who had this habit of constantly interrupting people, much to the annoyance of her acquaintances and friends, but I really believe she was completely unaware of the habit. She hadn't thought about changing because she didn't realize she needed to change. However, after taking my class on the meaning of dreams, her dreams soon remedied that situation. One day she stopped me as I was entering the church building, and said she just had to tell me a dream she had experienced several times. I had to smile when I heard the dream because it was a beautiful example of her subconscious showing her how her rudeness was driving people away. I just tried gently to hint at some things for her to consider, and I think she received some similar advice from her friends. Later on, I learned she had dropped her interest in dreams, so maybe she didn't really want to change after all.

I wanted to change because I wasn't happy with the life I was living. I looked into the mirror of the dream and saw what was reflected back to me. We all spend a certain amount of time each day checking our face for blemishes, making sure the hair is combed just right, and looking for unsightly particles of food trapped in the teeth. There was no glass mirror for getting an appraisal of my life, but I could look into my dreams and find it there. I'm sure that the total amount of time I spent on my appearance averaged at least fifteen minutes a day, so I thought my entire life was worth the effort I was putting into meditation and dream study.

THE PARADOX OF LOOKING

There is a bit of a paradox associated with looking. If I looked, I should do so with a clear mind to understand fully the message from the dream, but if I have a clear mind, why do I need to look at all? The dilemma was resolved by dream repetition and exaggeration. The repetition and exaggeration employed in my dreams eventually caused the dim view to brighten until the *aha* point was reached and the view became perfectly clear.

One dream scene mentioned earlier that I encounter when the message is not getting through to me is that of an overstuffed mailbox.

The mail has been delivered, but I am not collecting and reading it, so the message is lost. Simply put, the dream is saying that I am not getting the message even though it has been delivered repeatedly.

CHANGE BEGAN IN SMALL WAYS

My change was gradual and began in small ways, and as I received positive feedback, I made greater changes. When I dreamed that I was not in the right job, I did not think it would be a good idea to immediately quit my job and go home. There were times in my career when I was tempted to do just that, but I thought better of it. I didn't want to be sitting home for some time and find myself unable to pay bills. The same comment applies to the use of some of my intuitive insight. When I received what I thought was guidance to take some action, I made sure I evaluated the consequences and put it to the test. If it was something I really should do, there will be other urgings in that direction.

When I started listening for that still small voice, I realized I might be hearing my conscious thoughts and desires, or, worse yet, some fragment of my mind that was a result of a split in my personality due to unresolved issues. Psychics say that developing clairaudience is harder than clairvoyance because it is difficult, especially in the beginning, to separate this source from one's own self-talk or mind chatter. I have found this to be the case and still have times when I am not sure if I am engaging in self-talk or picking up a psychic message.

In 2013, I was following the NBA playoffs, and when the Miami Heat returned home down by one game for the final two games, I thought it was over for them. Before the first of the two games was played, one night just as I was entering sleep, a mental impression flashed across my mind. It was *Miami sweeps the final two games at home.* I wanted Miami to win, so I thought it might be wishful thinking on my part. This was not the case, as Miami did indeed sweep the remaining two games and won the championship.

I took small steps as change occurred; they are easier to correct when mistakes are made. In addition, I tried to avoid becoming so obsessed with dreams that they took over my life. I felt that my life is lived in the present, and my dreams could be a source of wisdom and guidance, but they could also become a problem if my life was not balanced. I learned that I should not be afraid to make a decision because I hadn't yet consulted my dreams or interpreted a dream with advice relating to the decision. I had to do the best I could at any given time with the information I had.

I avoided the addiction of spending so much time studying my dreams that I no longer had time to live the life they were trying to benefit. I had met people whose life became completely unbalanced because every waking moment was spent in a single activity, and I did not want my life to follow that path.

I have found that habits that were detrimental to my life in some way, such as a threat to my health or psychological well-being, were not isolated occurrences. As I began to work on a problem such as worrying or excessive snacking, I found myself becoming aware of other issues such as boredom and lack of job satisfaction. Sometimes the habit was just a response to stress in my life. Also, people often find that when they correct one habit, they simply substitute another one for the one given up. The ex-smoker suddenly puts on twenty pounds because the reason for the smoking has not been addressed. For real progress, I had to see the destructive habits or influences that existed in my life as part of a whole, not just as isolated events.

Sometimes we can have an enlightening experience just by reflecting on our lives or on something we have read. Many years ago, when I first started my professional career, I was a heavy smoker. My smoking was affecting my life to the point that it took the better part of an hour for me to stop coughing in the morning after I showered and prepared to start the day. It wasn't continuous coughing; it was more intermittent. However, it was a problem and concerned me. At that time of my life, I was not working with dreams or much of anything else along the lines of self-improvement or self-awareness.

One day I was thumbing through a *Reader's Digest* monthly issue when I discovered an article on cancer. The article was about various forms of cancer, but the ones that got my attention were the types of cancer that resulted from smoking. The description of cancer patients was graphic, like dreams, and I remember the description of a patient who held the cigarette to a hole in his throat to get his nicotine high because he could no longer breathe the smoke through his nose or mouth. The next day I quit smoking and never returned to it.

Now, in this case, I was able to have that *aha* moment when I realized deep down that I was going to be that man if I didn't take immediate action. No more rationalizing would work; I knew that for me smoking was done. I was convinced by the description and graphic nature of the image of the smoker who was so addicted that he would get the smoke into his lungs any way he could. Although in this case my image did not come through a dream, my dreams often served the same purpose and provided the same shock effect that I sometimes needed before I was ready to change.

I was disturbed by some of my dreams, maybe even terrified or panicked, but these jolts were sometimes necessary to get my attention. And when I awoke and saw that I was not nearly in the condition that I experienced in the dream, I gave a prayer of thanks that I was given an opportunity to act before it was too late. It was time to wake up, while the terrifying depiction of me or of the horrible situation in which I found myself was still a dream and not yet manifested in my physical life.

Our moods and emotions are constantly changing. If I have a dream showing me in a negative way, this does not mean that it is a statement about my entire life. And if I have a dream showing me making spiritual progress, this is not an affirmation that I have arrived at some highly evolved spiritual state. Whether a dream depicts me in a positive or negative way, the next day the situation could reverse. I am challenged every day, and my hope is that over time I am making progress.

I like to reflect upon the following analogy. When I first learned how to drive, my objective was to pass the driver's test and get a license. Naturally, I was quite careful and made a concerted effort to observe the signs and obey all the rules of the road. However, this did not mean that once I obtained my license I could become inattentive while driving on the highway and ignore all the laws. An effort has to be made every time I drive a car to avoid an accident. So whatever spiritual progress I think I have made is not a license for me to revert to old negative habits and no longer pay attention to what I am thinking and doing. I have to make that effort every day and continue to exercise what I learned that helped me progress in the first place.

Nine

CHALLENGES AND TRAGEDY

In addition to my exploration of the singles scene, after the dissolution of my marriage I began to refocus on my career. Even before the divorce, my dreams were showing me that I wasn't utilizing all my abilities in a purely technical position and were guiding me toward management. I began to take on project management responsibilities and after a few years transferred to a new start-up operation that was considered a sister division. In this new operation, after a few months I assumed a team leadership position, and within three years I was promoted to a management position, which included responsibility for supervising the activities of a group of analysts, software developers, and technicians. Over the subsequent years, it varied in size from a half dozen to nearly twenty, including contractors.

We developed some innovative applications during those years, and I found the environment both challenging and satisfying. I could honestly say that my job was becoming fun. I was both managing and enjoying what I was doing. My dreams had helped lead me into the right position for my abilities and temperament.

My dreams began to show me in different places that I did not recognize. Although the environments were unfamiliar, they held a degree of fascination in the dreams. Soon I began to travel to various domestic locations for meetings with prospects and customers. I didn't want to be on the road all the time, but I found my travel interesting, and it provided a nice change of pace. I liked visiting Phoenix, San Francisco, New Orleans, San Antonio, and many other cities I had not experienced before. In my previous job, most of my business trips had been to the Washington, D.C. area.

DREAMS HELP WITH CHALLENGES AT WORK

My job was not without challenges, and I had a constant stream of dreams related to situations at work. Emotional situations or unusual demands seemed to be a trigger and provided some of the strongest dreams, which were also the easiest to remember. I began to see patterns. If I dreamed about a situation that involved an emotional outburst or heated argument, I was certain that the following day would include a similar event. Upon awaking in the morning, I always reviewed my dreams to prepare me for the day. I checked for situations requiring my attention before I even arrived at work.

I recall a dream one night in which an enraged customer berated me. In the morning, I felt exhausted due to the traumatic dream confrontation. Later at work, I was sitting at my desk thinking about the dream and waiting for the call. By now, the pattern was familiar enough that I fully expected that I was going to have someone verbally attack me in an unforgettable way, but I was determined not to lose control. The call came, and I endured the rage that included screaming and name calling by the customer, having been prepared in advance by the dream.

I was fascinated by how accurately the events of the day could be reflected in my dreams from the previous night before I even thought about what I was going to do that day. I became comfortable with my dreams and began to rely upon them for added insight. This does not mean that I interpreted every dream correctly or heeded all the guidance from my dreams. And there were still days when I did not have any dream recall. On those days, I felt like I was naked. I was going forth not properly clothed.

A SIMPLE DREAM SOLVES A WORK-RELATED PROBLEM

In addition to preparing me for volatile situations at work, I received help for solving problems I encountered. I remember one period when I was struggling to find a solution to a problem at work without much success. Then I had a dream in which I was with a woman I knew who was wrapping a package. She quickly wrapped it up, complete with a ribbon tied into a neat bow. Because of the dream, I approached the woman to discuss my problem, and true to the dream, she made some suggestions that resulted in a quick solution to my dilemma.

I did not discuss my dream work and beliefs with my associates at work. I had learned from my previous job that not everyone is interested or receptive. In my solitary world, over the years I saw layoffs before they occurred, opportunities before they manifested, and changes that were underway but had not yet been presented to the employees. I continued to work in my capacity as a manger through the '80s and into the '90s. In the early '90s, my travel began to expand from domestic to international, something I had desired for a long time. I visited customers and prospects in Europe and provided support at trade shows. All of my dreams for career experiences were becoming realized.

A PROPHETIC DREAM REVEALS A TRAGEDY

In addition to work and my outside interests, during the '70s and '80s I spent time with my son and tried to monitor our relationship through my dreams. By high school, he had outgrown childhood hyperactivity and was trying to find his place in life. He was strong-willed and learned best through experience. Popular in his neighborhood, he had many friends, but also went through a rebellious teenage period. I came to realize that regardless of what I saw or felt there were lessons he had to learn for himself and that he would do some things I might regard as mistakes.

During this period, I had a dream that absolutely terrified me. I dreamed that I saw a young man who had just committed suicide. I was panicked. Aware of the high suicide rate among teenagers, I immediately focused on my son and his state of mind. At the time, he seemed to be happy and was in good spirits. I didn't see any signs that portended such a dire outcome. I couldn't think of anyone else who appeared on the verge of suicide. Then, a few nights later, I got a call that revealed that someone I knew, but with whom I had had no contact for several years, had committed suicide in the exact manner I saw in the dream. Unfortunately, I never made the connection to this person, so there was no opportunity to try to avert it. Although I did not make the connection, maybe my story will alert someone who has a similar dream to a situation where the proper connection is made and a life is saved.

AN UNHEEDED WARNING

In the early '90s, I was responsible for a project that I undertook with outside contractors that would change the quality of my life. Marketing wanted me to find or develop a new PC-based software product as an alternative to one of our mainframe products that they could offer to the marketplace. I did some research and performed evaluations that convinced me that we could not find an acceptable product that already existed. So I informed my boss that we would have to develop it, and that it would be a major undertaking. He gave me funding that I did not believe was adequate, but he said it was the best he could do. Furthermore, he said I could not hire anyone, so I was forced to employ outside contractors.

I still remember a disturbing dream I had about the project after deciding on an outside contractor. It did not say that it would be a failure, but it did suggest that there could potentially be problems with a major aspect of the development. I did not change course, despite the dream. At the time, I had no other options, and my boss and others were pressuring me to proceed. This position was familiar to me. A few times, when adding staff, I was directed to hire someone who I knew could, and probably would, lead to problems. In this case, I should have investigated further, but I didn't. The project consumed several years of my life, hurt my reputation within the company, and stressed me to the limit.

The product was released late, but it did achieve a capability that none of our competitors' products had. However, the delay took its toll, and my boss decided to have me replaced as manager of the group and to focus all my efforts on a program to support a new product under development. I saw this change unfold very clearly in a dream weeks before he announced his decision. In the dream, he and others were discussing what to do with what he saw as a troubled group under his control. In the dream, the decision was made to implement the change I described.

DREAMS PREPARED ME FOR THE UNEXPECTED

After leaving my job as manager of the applications group, I briefly held several positions before becoming manager of a new group that was similar to the group I had previously managed. The old applications group was now part of engineering. I performed in this role for several years before retiring. We did not do any development, but we did affect the development that was done. In this role, I was mainly focused on helping our salespeople penetrate new markets. As part of my job, I made presentations on workflow to executives from companies all over the world who visited our facility.

My dreams were invaluable because they prepared me the night before for how my presentation would be received. This allowed me to make adjustments in some cases, and in all cases prepared me mentally for what was coming. Rather than being caught off-guard, I was prepared ahead of time for a difficult meeting and hostile or unreasonable participants.

I worked for several years as manager of the workflow group before I retired in 2008. Even before retirement, I wanted to get back to my dream book and pursue publication of my short stories. I now had a vast amount of experience in working with dreams, and I believed it would require considerable focus and effort to write the books I envisioned about my prophetic experiences. I would also need time to prepare my short stories for publication, and retirement would provide this opportunity.

Ten

THE ROAD SELDOM TAKEN

CHANGE WAS HARD

There is an overwhelming array of books, magazine articles, talk shows, infomercials, religious organizations, educational programs, and self-help groups ready to help a person change his life and achieve maximum potential. In my early years of seeking, I investigated many of them. However, despite all of this help, the physical and psychological well-being of Americans as a whole seems to be in a woeful state. The incidence of diseases like diabetes is exploding, and there is mass addiction to drugs, both legal and illegal. Depression is widespread, and teenage suicides have skyrocketed in a nation with more material wealth than any nation in the history of the world.

So what is wrong? Why aren't these sources of help making great improvements in the quality of life? I think the answer is simple: Implementing real change is a hard thing for people to do. It was certainly hard for me. During an earlier period in my life, when I was giving a lecture to a church group, one individual criticized me during an open discussion with the comment, "Why do you make it so hard? All you have to do is believe in Jesus Christ." Well, maybe that is true depending on what was meant by "believe," but if it were such an easy thing to do, I don't think we would see all the problems that exist today, even among church members.

I found that changing my fundamental beliefs was a difficult thing to do and required extraordinary awareness of myself, not as I would like to be or thought I was, but as I actually was. There is a story told by Jiddu Krishnamurti in *Freedom from the Known* concerning awareness that I have never forgotten. He was traveling by car in India with a chauffeur and several other men. The men were so busy discussing awareness that they were unaware that the driver had hit a goat in the road. When it was brought to their attention, they were completely surprised. I thought about this story many times when I was tempted to think I had become self-aware.

Through meditation and my dreams, I became increasingly aware that talk is not the thing. I have heard people talk about believing in Jesus Christ, Buddha, the Koran, or something else, but all their talk doesn't seem to get at the essence of the truth they are trying to relate. In fact, it is when there is no talk, as in meditation, when the mind is not engaged in inner or outer talk, that I have experienced something profound that gives true meaning to everything else.

CHANGE REQUIRED COMMITMENT

I think the implementation of real change in one's life requires extraordinary commitment. My best promises sometimes quickly evaporated when I stepped back into a difficult job, a disintegrating marriage, financial hardships, betrayal, or any one of many other challenges I experienced in the real world. A seriously ill child or spouse will test the beliefs of even the most faithful. As a toddler, my son was admitted to the hospital for allergy testing. His condition started to deteriorate rapidly, and in a matter of a few days, his condition approached the critical stage. My wife called me from the hospital and told me to prepare for the worst. I had thought my faith had made great strides, until I had been put to the test and discovered how far I had to go.

While at the hospital, after long hours of waiting, I became so tired I briefly dozed off. I had a dream showing my son recovered and back home playing with his toys. And with the help of a new doctor, this occurred. But prior to his recovery, everything I thought I had learned seemed distant and without significance when faced with his loss.

While the concept of change and the description of a process to follow to enable change may be simple, I found that implementation could be difficult to achieve with many failures and false starts along the way. It is easy to sit with friends sipping coffee in a comfortable environment talking about truth, beauty, love, and seeing the good in everyone. It is far different when we encounter the slums or that person who lies to us, steals from us, or does us physical harm.

Change was not easy for me, but I decided it was necessary and persevered. And I think I have been more successful in working with dreams than most people have because I *worked* with dreams. Despite my failures, I continued; I did not give up when I had an unflattering dream, or was shown that I was at fault in some situation. I was patient and prepared for the long haul. And as I stated earlier, my dreams previewing the next day did not fully develop until I had resolved some important issues in my life. Despite what some claim, I didn't find any instant solution to my problems. I had to work through them when and where they occurred, before I could move on to the next level. I don't think a person who hates his neighbor or members of his own family is going to be successful in finding Nirvana through meditation, dreams, or some other means. The hate must first be resolved before progress can be made.

THE ROAD SELDOM TAKEN

I have collected my thoughts into an approach for dealing with life's challenges that I followed based on prayer, meditation, and dreams. I share the approach with others who may find some aspects of it of benefit in their own lives. This approach is not a new program or process for enlightenment. Instead, the tools and methods involved have been there for a long time, but are on *the road seldom taken.*

I am always amazed that meditation and dreams, so prevalent in the Bible and at the foundation of other religions, do not find their way into the programs and teachings of organized religion. There are some notable exceptions, such as Unity, but for most people meditation and dreams seem to be just something in the Bible or other holy book, without a direct relationship to their daily lives. Inspiration and guidance from dreams did not end with the New Testament; I have found help and illumination from dreams to be an integral part of my life as a human being.

And meditation has always been the way to enter into direct communion with the Universal Consciousness.

Psychologists and psychiatrists employ dreams as a way to understand the psyche of the individual seeking help. When I started working with dreams, I did not believe that the province of dreams was theirs alone to explore and understand; I believed that I was the person best qualified to understand my own dreams. This might not be the case for the seriously psychologically disturbed, but I did not see myself in that position. I have not found a better tool as a window into the subconscious and its awesome power and resources, and I can't think of a better source of guidance in my daily life.

FREEDOM FROM FEAR

The road seldom taken is not always an easy road, but this road can free a person from the fears and concerns of life. Powerful tools and resources are at the person's disposal to solve problems and make good decisions. Rather than being at the whim of fortune and forced to deal with issues that seem to spring from nowhere in a random way, through dreams and meditation I found a means to create my personal reality and deal effectively with any situation I encountered. I discovered that I was not alone, but was connected to everyone else and to a Universal Consciousness. As a result, my fears and concerns began to drop away.

Some say that if we know what will happen, it takes all the joy and mystery out of life. I have not found this to be the case. I still had plenty of opportunity for surprise and for the spontaneous to occur; I simply enlarged my awareness to include the subconscious as well.

PRAYER FOR ATUNEMENT

The road seldom taken is not a rigid procedure, but a simple process that involves the use of the methods I followed to deal with daily existence. This process includes material that was covered in earlier chapters, but it is summarized and integrated here as what I found to be a unified approach to life.

This means several things. First, prayer became a part of my life. One of the best books I have found on the subject is *The Soul's Sincere Desire* by Glenn Clark. Do not be put off with the thought that by "prayer" I am talking about making some entreaty to a higher power to do something for me. I am referring to the effort made by my conscious mind to attune itself to the oneness of all life, which can be contemplation of being a channel of help to those I serve, a smile for someone who is down in spirit, or recognition of the life force in everyone. It is an attitude and not just saying certain words or repeating certain phrases. For me prayer is not at a set time but can be employed at any time and in any circumstance. It is often just an appreciation for the creator of the beauty and grandeur of nature, as I overlook a setting from a highway or state park.

MEDITATION FOR LISTENING

I have found the practice of meditation critical for getting the maximum benefit from life and the best guidance from my dreams. As opposed to prayer during which the conscious mind is active, meditation is freeing or quieting the mind so the Eternal One can manifest directly in my consciousness. Meditation usually requires more discipline, and I found that I needed to set aside fifteen or more—I strived for thirty—minutes in the morning before I plunged into the day's activities. If I waited, even with the best of intentions, I found that the day slipped away and I never got around to meditating. And I really needed the period of meditation to carry me through the challenges of the day.

This does not mean that I made it a rigid process to try to force the mind to be quiet—that would quickly become onerous and unsuccessful. I tried to make it a time of peace and joy, in order to establish a sense of attunement before I became embroiled in the day's activities. Through observation of thoughts and their release, I found that the mind would naturally become quiet, and eventually that presence I sought was there. Some people prefer to meditate later in the day before retiring for the evening. I had to find what worked best for me. I found that one difficulty with the late-evening meditation was the struggle to stay awake after being tired from a long day. And without a morning meditation, my day's activities would not have benefited from the sense of attunement. As circumstances permitted, I also had brief meditations during the day.

A long time ago, I was sitting in my office at work with the door closed, trying to finish a report without interruption, when my mind starting thinking about something I had read the night before from one of the Krishnamurti dialogues. I suddenly understood what he was saying, and I let go of my immediate concerns. My thoughts and problems fell away. Then, in an instant, my consciousness shifted from my office to somewhere else. In a trance,

I became aware of all my relatives who had passed over, and I knew, with a deep sense of freedom, that life wasn't about money or wealth at all. This all occurred in a brief span of time.

Another time I was in California on business, seated at a table in a restaurant with business colleagues. We were getting ready to order when a strange, peaceful feeling began to sweep over me. It grew in intensity and left me buoyant with joy and feeling completely in harmony with life, to the point that I was barely able to contain myself. The presence I felt lasted for a long time, and my mind was somewhere else for most of the dinner.

DREAMS FOR GUIDANCE

I have found my dreams to be extremely important. They offered a solution for the majority of my problems, but most people totally neglect them as a source of practical help or inspiration. For real progress with dreams, I realized I needed to get a notebook and start recording my dreams. I quickly found that dreams and meditation are not separate from each other. My periods of meditation heightened my dream recall, content, and guidance. My dreams better reflected my spiritual progress and provided feedback that allowed me to make corrections quickly when I got on the wrong path.

On *the road seldom taken*, I was working with all three areas: prayer, meditation, and dreams. This obviously required some seriousness on my part; it required a commitment of time. I did not find this commitment to be burdensome. I was easily spending wasted time each day in idle gossip or watching TV programs of little benefit. And I devoted considerable time and energy each day in a nonconstructive way worrying about my job, finances, health, family, and numerous other concerns. In my early life, I spent long hours trying to dig myself out of situations I would have avoided if I had been on *the road seldom taken* all along. One wrong decision can take years to correct, if it can be corrected at all. The influences of our decisions can last a lifetime and can affect our family and friends as well as us. They certainly did in my case.

The most effective people are the most effective at the utilization of time; they seem to accomplish more each day than their less effective counterparts do. I decided that at least fifteen minutes—preferably thirty—a day for regular meditation and another fifteen minutes a day to record my dreams was a very effective use of my time. Once the dreams were recorded, I could review and study them at my leisure. A half hour up to forty-five minutes a day didn't seem like much to me when it had the potential to save me hundreds or even thousands of hours of grief and made my life far richer and more interesting at the same time, in addition to helping me avoid lost opportunities.

CAVEATS

There are some caveats I would like to share that saved me from grief as I started to make the changes I described. Some of these are mentioned in earlier chapters, but are included here as well, so that there is a complete reference in one place. When I awake in the morning, I quickly review the dreams I can remember before getting up. I do this to make sure they are firmly set in conscious memory. If I get up first, I will most likely lose some or all of them. Of course, the best way to keep them is to record them right away, but this did not work well for me. In the beginning, I would record one or two word associations that would help me remember when I was ready to enter the detail into my notebook. Now, after many years of working with dreams, I focus on the dream after I become aware of it, and then I go back sleep. Usually, I can recall it in the morning. I try to record the dream content even before I have the morning meditation.

When I meditate, I do not follow some rigid technique or think I need to have certain experiences for success. This is a quiet time for me to listen for that *still small voice* and for me to feel that sense of connection with the Universal. I set this as my ideal as I enter into meditation. The conscious mind often does not want to cooperate, and I sometimes find my mind filled with chatter, especially if I have pressing issues to address. I try to be patient and just let the chatter and images pass by. I become the observer and just observe, without any attempt to suppress or to become involved or identified with a particular thought. Normally, my mind quiets down naturally. After I have captured my dreams and meditated, I am ready to face the day.

As the day evolves, I am alert to what is going on in my mind, and when I have a free moment over coffee or lunch, I reflect on my dreams from the previous night. When I was employed in a corporate job, I tried to do this several times during the day, which included my drive to work and back home. My dreams were about me, and some were concerned with the day's activities, so I tried not to ignore them until the end of the day. By then I would be in the situation where I wished I had paid attention to one of my dreams earlier. At the end of the day, I reviewed my dreams to see how they related to the current day. This is where I started to see the pattern of precognition as it unfolded.

As I began to see some of the remarkable dreams that can occur, related to precognition or something else, I became extremely enthusiastic about what I had discovered and wanted to share it with everyone else. Unfortunately, not everyone shared my enthusiasm; some became downright hostile if I continued to press them about dreams. As I previously described in one of my experiences, the individual did not want to know anything about dreams, even if everything I said was true. I believe this reaction is typical when someone thinks bad news is likely.

We all know that we may be doing some things that we shouldn't and aren't doing some things we should, but we don't want to be shown these shortcomings in our dreams. (These are usually referred to as the sins of commission and omission.) If I take an exam for a course in school and am concerned about my performance, I am usually not eager to get my test results. When I expect bad or unpleasant news, often I would rather not know.

Finally, I tried to avoid becoming sullen or discouraged by presumed lack of progress. I reminded myself that there is no timetable. I was doing work at a subconscious level, even if I had not yet experienced conscious progress. On the other hand, I didn't procrastinate to the point that I was just dabbling with an occasional meditation or looking at an occasional dream that I found interesting. I saw other people take this approach and not make much progress, so I decided that I would make a serious effort to see what was possible.

We are in a society and age that expects things to happen instantly. The fast food at one of the popular burger restaurants, the rush from one school activity to another, the text messages, the social networking, the movie downloads, and a host of other regular activities are geared toward a fast-paced, hectic lifestyle that is often at odds with the path I took. What I learned on *the road seldom taken* is about quality and meaning, not speed and diversion. For me, it was about the quality and meaning of life, not about the number of activities I could cram into a single day.

The addiction to our technology has become so great we have to pass laws to prevent people from text messaging while driving a car. I believe that dreams of warning, which can graphically show the dreamer's life ended on a highway by a poor decision that could easily be corrected, is one way to get the person's attention and prevent the pain and suffering that result from something easily avoided.

The road seldom taken has its own twists and turns, but overall I found it smoother and much easier to traverse than other roads that contain steep embankments, sudden curves, and falling debris with no warnings posted. *The road seldom taken* did not prevent me from facing challenges in my life, but I found it much easier to navigate than the alternatives. I have avoided many situations that would have ended badly, and found direction and opportunities that I am quite sure I would have missed if I had not taken this road early in my career. *The road seldom taken* became a road of hope and confidence with unlimited possibilities for me to create my own destiny. I chose this road while in the first study group in Florida, and it was contrary to what I was taught and experienced while growing up.

I was born into a family with a propensity to worry. My mother worried about money like many people, which was not surprising since we were quite poor, but she also worried about the weather, about what might happen tomorrow, next week, and next month or year. I think much of it was learned behavior from her father, who worried every bit as much, if not more than my mother did. They rarely looked at what might go right, but always imagined all the things that could go wrong. This was probably because they did not have a safety net, and the slightest unexpected expense could mean not eating or not paying some bill.

Their propensity to worry is probably why my grandfather reacted negatively when I told him I was considering college as an option. In his view, this was beyond my station in life because no one in our family had ever graduated from college. He simply was not constituted to see how it could be positive and worth pursuing and immediately looked for the downside. For him, we were locked into a future that would play out regardless of what we thought or tried to do. And in his mind, the future I was locked into did not include college. I decided to ignore his advice and attended college, graduating in four years as a member of the Phi Beta Kappa Society.

During my years of working with dreams, I still had to do my homework and consider possible consequences of my actions, but after making my decision, I focused on a positive outcome and worked hard to make it a reality. I believe that worry is both counterproductive and enervating. If I was on the wrong path, I discovered that my dreams would tell me. And if I was on the right path, my dreams confirmed my choice and actions as correct.

MANAGING MY TIME

In concluding this chapter, I would like to make a final point about how I allocated my time each day. Earlier, I said that I spent a half hour or more devoted to meditation and a review of dreams. I normally meditated in the morning. Otherwise, while at work, I quickly became embroiled in situations that caused me to lose focus and slide into a negative frame of mind. I also discovered that it was easy to become negative in the evening, when the national or world news and network shows are on television.

After a long day at work, sometimes I just turned on the television set and started watching whatever was on without regard to content or quality. I found some good programming, particularly on the educational channels, but I also discovered that many of the programs were not worth watching. Sometimes, after watching the evening news, it would take me several hours to regain a positive outlook. So I became much more selective in what I watched, and I suddenly found myself feeling better with a lot more time.

Eleven

THE TIME PARADOX

The concept of time is a key part of my story because by its very definition a precognitive dream involves time. The nature of time fascinated me, which is probably the reason I was initially attracted to precognitive dreams. The telling of my story requires a further investigation of this concept because there is a way of viewing time that might explain why and how precognitive dreams occur. Since many of my dreams were of this type, I wanted to understand why this was the case. And I wanted to understand the nature of a future existing before I lived it. The ramifications of this were enormous and affected how I saw my life on earth and man in relation to the cosmos.

TWO COMMON WAYS TO VIEW TIME

Time is normally considered a basic concept that is intuitively obvious. The great Sir Isaac Newton took the concept of time to be something universal and absolute. However, Albert Einstein showed that this was not the case and that the passage of time as measured by an observer was dependent upon the motion of the observer. Two observers in motion relative to each other could obtain different measures for the time elapse of an event. Philosophers have also worried about the meaning of time, and many different theories have evolved. I found that there are two major approaches to understanding time, and their treatment of time is vastly different.

In one approach, which is closest to what is commonly believed, time is something fixed, and events exist in time when they occur and not before. The past is fixed, but the future is open and undetermined until the possibilities collapse into the one selected and the past meets the future in the now. If I attend a class tomorrow, the event does not exist until it occurs the next day. Today it is only one of many possibilities and does not yet exist. The possibilities have no reality of their own.

In the approach favored by scientists, every becoming already exists. The past, present, and future already exist in a four-dimensional space-time continuum. The laws of physics work just as well in reverse as they do moving forward in time. The now of an event depends upon the observer. What I see as happening now can be seen as happening in the past or future by another observer. Events that are simultaneous to one observer may not be to another observer. Now for most people, this view is not very satisfying. The typical person cannot be convinced that events exist in his life before they occur or that they are somehow fixed in a rigid and absolute sense. Then there are the numerous questions and paradoxes that always arise about the possibility of traveling back in time to change the present or future. No lack of possibilities has arisen from these considerations.

My purpose is not to go into detail about the approaches to time, but instead to point out that much of what we take as given is no longer considered obvious and, in some cases, is the subject of serious scientific investigation. The scientific view supports time travel into the future, but not into the past due to paradoxes that would be created if this were possible. So what is happening in prophecy or precognitive dreams? Am I traveling through time when I see the future, or am I logically deducing what will happen based on my conscious knowledge and a subconscious connection to other minds? If I subconsciously knew what everyone else planned to do the next day, then unexpected events seen the night before in my dreams could be logically deduced. Of course, this would not be possible if people were truly making largely spontaneous decisions from moment to moment.

Let's consider the dream in which I encountered my boss at work Monday morning with a severe case of an allergic reaction due to poison from a plant. Now, if my subconscious linked to his and tuned into his anguish and physical rash on a subconscious level, I could experience that in a dream the night before. So was my dream truly precognitive? The same can probably be said of most precognitive dreams, but it requires an enormous amount of knowledge down to intricate details and an extraordinary coordination of events from an almost infinite number of sources. In other words, my subconscious would have to know what other people and nature intended to do from moment to moment. If many decisions were unplanned and made spontaneously, as most people believe, this would not be possible. Perhaps I am seeing the most probable scenario after everything and everyone is taken into account. This alone would be quite fantastic.

A DIFFERENT WAY TO VIEW TIME

My dreams and some of the metaphysical teachings from sources like Seth, Jane Roberts's trance essence, suggest a modified view of what scientists believe. In this view, many futures exist in alternate realities, but as probable versions as far as physical manifestations are concerned. One of the futures that exist in another reality can be selected in the present for physical manifestation.

Another way to say it is that the future doesn't just happen; we select the future that we want to become part of our physical experience. The present is all-important because from the present we determine the future we experience. However, the future, unlike the common view, already exists as one of a multitude of possibilities that all have a real existence in other realities. The subconscious has a hand in selecting the one that will find physical expression. Things we experience don't just happen, but have already happened on a psychic level.

In dreams, we work out the scenario that is enacted the next day and beyond. I select from the possibilities and collapse them into the events that become physically manifested the following day. It is like moving from one parallel reality to another to select content that makes up what we choose as our lives. There are many branches to the tree. We pick the branches that become physical reality as our lives.

As an analogy in two dimensions, suppose I take a reel of film or a digital file that represents a movie. Now consider each frame that represents a scene at some instant. These scenes all already exist, and I can select or recombine them in different ways to change the movie. Maybe I have some additional scenes that weren't used that allow me to create a different ending. Now I add to this picture by making the scenes three-dimensional and inserting myself into the scenes. While the scenes are being selected, projected in the case of movie film or digitally displayed from a file, suppose I have the opportunity to make some script changes before the selection occurs. So I decide, I don't want this scene next; I want to replace it with another one. And each scene I select leads to a number of choices for the next one. Although greatly simplified, this should give some sense of what is happening based on this modified view of time.

My point is that in this view time does not exist; there is just a set of scenes or possibilities. And I not only select scenes; I am in the scenes. In the case of a movie, the experience of time happens when I project or display the scenes at a certain rate on a screen or monitor. The inability of the eye and brain to separate the scenes when the movie is played gives the illusion of time, of continuity, but all the scenes already exist as fixed, discrete captures. In the physical life we live, the illusion of time is a result of our physiological structure.

As I live my life each day, I am experiencing preselected events in a sequence and way that is compatible with physical reality and my physiological structure, and the illusion of time results. It is seamless and real, just like the movie. The world I see is real to me because I have created the world I see and live in. If I want a different world, it must begin in my mind, so different possibilities are selected by the subconscious as it attempts to build the world I have told it I want. I tell it every time I talk to myself, with every suggestion to myself that I look good or bad, that I love, deserve love, am or am not a good person. The world that is *real* to me is the one I create.

The good news is that if I don't like the one I see, or the situation in which I find myself, I can change it. In the present, I can always change the future that is manifested as reality. It does mean that it may take some real effort on my part to break from the existing pattern because it may be deep within my subconscious.

In one case, when I was trying to make a change in my behavior, I was told in a dream that it would be difficult because of the deep channels in my subconscious that supported the old behavior. However, I can start by seeing the patterns in my life through observation of myself and of my thoughts and actions, and by interpreting my dreams, which gives me a window into my subconscious. It is counterproductive if I start beating up and criticizing myself because I see things that I don't like. The purpose of my observation is to learn what I really think and do, not to judge it. More on this process can be found in *The Power of Now* and in the writings of J. Krishnamurti. Both spiritual teachers have influenced me.

Now, this may sound crazy to some, but this modified view of time is what I have found in working with my dreams for many years. Sometimes the detail in the dream is so normal and clear that it seems like I have woken up, gone to wherever the dream is taking place, and acted out the part, but I wake up and realize I was dreaming and haven't left my bed. Then, as the day unfolds, I live it exactly as I had in the dream, even when many situations and events that occur were unplanned and appear to be spontaneous. These occurrences have changed the way I view life, time, and my purpose on this earth. They have changed how I see my future and the future of the planet.

PROPHECY AND THE FUTURE

Prophecy has long been part of the culture, dating back to ancient times and the Greek oracle at Delphi. Often, people who are unfulfilled in the present hope to find happiness in the future through wealth, a better job, a more satisfying relationship, or by finding God. And those who have great material wealth worry about what the future will bring that might rob them of their possessions.

There is always that uneasiness about what may be lurking around the corner to ruin what one has worked hard to establish. However, through dreams and meditation, I found that the future doesn't just spring unexpected events upon me. The probable events already exist, and I have, in an intimate way, a hand in creating their physical reality. Now, this does not mean that I can control the destiny of the world or every event in my own life. Since everyone is feeding thoughts into a universal consciousness, I believe mass events are determined by the many, and the destiny of the world is a cooperative effort. The reality of cities, states, and nations, as well as nature, is determined by the mass consciousness of the inhabitants.

If I see the next day's events in my dreams, can I change those events? Can I cause something else to occur with that knowledge as I begin the day? I asked myself these questions repeatedly as I encountered my precognitive dreams. As a concrete example, suppose I dream that I am going to have an argument with someone at work the next day. Can I prevent that argument from happening, or am I destined to watch it play out? The answer is not simple because I found that it depends on my level of self-awareness.

In the beginning, I discovered that despite my best efforts I would be through the encounter before I remembered the dream. It is as if I was pulled into a vortex that wouldn't let me out until all of the events previewed the night before had played out. However, as my self-awareness improved, there were situations that I have been able to avoid or modify, but I simultaneously had to be very aware of the information from my dreams and what was happening around me.

The events in my dream that foreshadow the next day are taking place on a psychic level before they manifest in the physical world, and they are highly energized. As a result, it took great awareness and effort to change the script that had been written by me the night before.

WE HAVE LESS CONTROL OVER GLOBAL EVENTS

Events that are more global in nature are even more difficult to influence because the outcome is the result of energy from a large number of sources. If I start feeding positive energy into a global situation such as a natural disaster, war, or political event, my effect may be small, but the combined effort of many, which may not even be a large number, can be substantial. So if I see a view of the future that extends beyond my individual life, such as an earthquake or sudden downturn in the stock market, I have found that it is very likely to happen if it is a close event. If the event is in the more distant future, there is still the possibility that changes in consciousness will result in a different outcome or delay the outcome I have seen.

Global warming is a good example of this. Scientists believe there is global warming, and that man has either caused or exacerbated this phenomena. However, not everyone agrees. Many believe that there is no global warming, and even if there is, they see little threat to our lives. The outcome is not cast in concrete as an event that can be predicted with certainty. There are many possible outcomes, ranging from no substantial impact on our lives to cataclysmic earth changes.

With vision, one can see the probable outcome, but nature and the exercise of the free will of the combined populace will determine the actual outcome. This is why prophets who claim to see the future cannot be certain that an event will occur; only that it is highly likely. For the same reason, if I see a future event through meditation or my dreams, there is no guarantee that it will occur. I believe it will most likely occur unless I or someone else makes a change in direction that causes a change in the probable outcome.

There are individuals today, who claim to have prophetic visions through dreams and trance states, who are publishing their views of the future.

A MODERN-DAY NOSTRADAMUS

Gordon-Michael Scallion is one such individual. He is a controversial figure who is considered by some to be a modern-day Nostradamus. As a result of a health crisis in 1979, Mr. Scallion claims that he became aware of a presence that was to change the entire course of his life. He said he developed paranormal abilities that enlarged his view of everything he had thought and believed. With his new abilities, he was able to see a light or aura around people, his dreams became prophetic, and he became aware of a source for guidance or his higher self, referred to by Edgar Cayce as the superconscious.

GLOBAL EARTH CHANGES

In the beginning of the change after his illness, Mr. Scallion had horrible, upsetting dreams of natural disasters on a global scale. These occurred night after night, and were not something he could ignore or put out of his mind. He eventually concluded that he was being shown probable changes in the face of the earth, with entire coastlines and countries being altered. These dreams led him to the creation of a map that showed the United States, and later the world, after the changes occur. In his original map, he showed most of these changes happening prior to the year 1997.

However, the drastic changes depicted did not occur, and many wrote him off as a fraud. So does this mean he was wrong, just another prophet of doom? In his case, I'm not certain he was wrong about the outcome, but the timing was clearly wrong. As I mentioned earlier, outcomes can be changed or delayed. Concerning his predictions of earth changes, I think that they might just have been delayed.

There are two reasons for this belief. The first relates to a dream I had as a teenager in which I saw the entire course my life would take. Near the end of that dream, which was definitely in the later years of my life, I witnessed events that included monumental earth changes of the scale predicted by Mr. Scallion. The second reason is the effect that civilization is having on the earth concerning global warming. Scientists believe that man is exacerbating some of the changes in climate due to natural cycles, which could potentially result in cataclysmic change. The September 2013 draft report from the United Nations on climate changes points to man as the likely main cause of global warming since the mid-20th century.

Mr. Scallion is not alone in his visions of dramatically altered continents and coastlines in the future. Others, through their sources of guidance, have also produced maps based on their visions of the future earth. The other maps I have seen are not identical, but resemble the ones produced by Mr. Scallion. The reasons stated for the changes are similar and involve a combination of natural cycles and man-made effects.

WHY I CARE

I am not a prophet of doom or even a prophet at all. And I do not believe the world will end any time soon. Most of what I see concerning the future relates to my life and to those close to me, and occasionally I see an event with broader ramifications. However, there are trends clearly visible to scientists that indicate that disturbing changes are occurring on our planet. One can argue that changes always occur and someone is always calling for the end of the world, so why worry about it. Yes, change is natural. Entire continents have changed size and location in the past, as well as the magnetic field and polarity of the earth. However, changes can be accelerated or made worse in their effect, so do we really want to ignore the effect man is having on the earth? Do we want to ignore man's role in determining the future of the planet?

Some twenty years ago, I was in a coastal city on a business trip with an overnight stay. That night I had a brief dream in which I heard a voice that said the following: *"When the earth axis shifts, this area will not be safe. It will be inundated."* I take this dream very seriously. In all other occurrences of dreams of this type, I have never had a message delivered by a voice that did not prove to be accurate. And I have had many over the years. Scientists know that major, potentially catastrophic changes will occur in the future. The question is not if, but when. Maybe people think it is so far in the future that it isn't worth their concern. Someday the inhabitants of the earth will not be so lucky.

The future is unknown, but certain scenarios may be very probable. I believe we create the future from the present, but often the present is just a continuation of the past. I can help create the future by really being in the present, by being aware of what I am thinking and doing from moment to moment. Through this self-awareness in the now, through feedback and guidance from my dreams, I can change my future and help change the future of the planet as well. I could say that I don't care, that I don't want to know. However, time will grind on and events will be born into my life, whether I am aware or not. They just may not be what I desire or what is most beneficial or fulfilling for my experience on this earth.

One might argue that the whole point of prophecy is to get people to change so the events prophesied do not take place. If a prophet is proven wrong, most people will say he was just another lunatic whose ramblings were nonsense. However, the truth might be far different. It might be that enough people listened and acted to change the probable outcome, so the prophesied event did not occur. And the prophet accomplished his mission.

Twelve

Final Thoughts

In this book, I have told the story of my work with meditation and dreams, which included how they provided me with daily guidance. With numerous examples taken from my life, I have showed how I used information from dreams to make major changes that led to a more satisfying life. The aspects of my life that were affected encompassed the physical, mental, and spiritual realms. While it may be easy to understand the relationship between a specific dream and the changes I made concerning my health or job, the effect the dreams had on my mental state is more subtle.

Prior to my work with dreams, I had extensive education and training in scientific disciplines. My view of the universe was based on what I learned in my physics courses, and in many respects, it was quite rigid. I did have the sometimes uneasy sense from exposure to my mother's premonitions during my youth that maybe there was a lot more to the universe than what I had been taught and what was the province of science. However, I did not dwell on any of her experiences and relegated them to the background of my consciousness. In college, I took some courses in philosophy, but I was not persuaded by any of the arguments to change my thinking in any major way.

As I began to study Edgar Cayce, I became a voracious reader of some of the major metaphysical works. Later, I examined the Seth material channeled by Jane Roberts and worked through lessons from *A Course in Miracles*. I wanted to see if there was a consensus view that would explain the meaning of life. And as I began to work with my dreams, I wanted to understand how I could see my future in a dream. At that time—and still today—many scientists consider anything relating to the psychic as nonsense, a fraud perpetrated on the gullible. However, I had my dreams and my psychic experiences. These were as real to me as are any of the physical objects I deal with every day. So I continued my work with dreams and decided that I would be on a solitary path for much of the time, especially when I was at my job in the corporate world.

As I applied what I learned and continued my study of classic works like *The Law of Psychic Phenomena*, my view of the world began to change. I realized that I had just scratched a tiny bit of the surface of a greater reality, but I saw enough to convince me that some of the beliefs I had developed during the first twenty-five years of my life needed a radical revision. I knew that what people like Edgar Cayce were saying was true in least some respects because I could see it in my own life. And as the years passed, my reality moved ever closer to a metaphysical view of the universe.

The change in my view of life and my enhanced awareness through meditation and dreams have been isolating at times. In my job, my views could not be openly expressed, as I stated earlier. And today, I find that much of society is moving in a direction that is <u>at odds with how I am living and what I find beneficial</u>. I think that doing things more quickly and efficiently can be good, but my conscious mind has limits and my inner needs can't be ignored. And a society totally enamored with the latest technology and devices seems to have little interest in one's inner needs.

THE PACE OF CHANGE

We live in an interesting time, as we see major changes taking place in technology. The pace of change, though, is at times overwhelming. I learn about and adjust to one new technology only to find that it is already being replaced by something else. And I do not see this trend slowing and often ask myself if it is improving the quality of my life and the lives of people around me. The PC, tablet, and mobile phone are now considered indispensable, and the way people communicate and interact is forever changed; however, I'm not sure the quality of life has made the same strides forward.

When I tell young people how I conducted business early in my career, they look at me in disbelief. My work career spans a period that began before the invention of the PC and ended with most of the tools we see today. In the early years of my career, my company's customers would order software and digital fonts stored on IBM punched cards through a group I managed. I would receive a fax or an order for shipment of a standard product in six to ten days. We also did a lot of custom work, and some of these jobs were quoted with delivery times of three or four weeks. If a customer needed a standard product right away, we would ship it through one of the overnight carriers for delivery next day. However, this was rare; most rush orders were second-day delivery.

As the years progressed, the IBM punched cards were replaced by magnetic tape as technology and customers' expectations changed. Then the PC started having an impact, and many of our programs migrated to this platform. And with the advances in technology, the software products and fonts we sold could easily be provided to customers as digital files through communication links. Our customers started requesting that we send them the files by the end of the day. That was fine for a while, but then they decided that they couldn't wait that long and would request delivery in two hours. Finally, the technology reached a point where they could access a partition on a server the IT Department reserved for customers, and they wanted access to the files within five or ten minutes. I can still recall some of the requests that started out saying, "I want you to immediately..." And I would often receive calls that began with someone saying, "It's been ten minutes. Where is it?"

I need balance in my life. I don't want technology to take over my life; I want technology to enhance my life. I find that sometimes the timesaving devices can create other, more serious problems concerning human behavior. I don't want to become enslaved by man's creations; I want to be freed from many of the mundane tasks I have to perform. My inner needs are of primary importance to me. I feel best around nature, when I can have a quiet time to experience that sense of attunement, that sense of oneness. My goal is to reduce mind chatter, and I often feel that this is inconsistent with the direction taken by the broader society, which is fascinated by and completely absorbed in the new technology.

MY DREAMS PROVIDED BALANCE AND
WHOLENESS

As I stated in the beginning of the book, everyone dreams, even if the dreams are not remembered. Research has shown that dreaming is necessary for the health of the individual, and interrupted dreams can result in behavior problems. Unfortunately, even if not interrupted, most people don't realize the full benefit of their dreams because they don't recall and act upon them. When my conscious mind was cut off from the subconscious, the quality of my life suffered as a result. I was leading a fragmented, unbalanced life that was separate from the greater whole of my individuality and the source of my being. I was closed to my own greater purpose. The guidance from my dreams provided the balance and wholeness that I needed in my life.

The downside of some modern technology is that it increases the chatter of minds that are already filled with self-talk, with little time spent listening. I think the current trend is to spend less time trying to reconnect with the subconscious and more time absorbed in the new devices. As Eckhart Tolle and other spiritual teachers point out, the problem is not that there is too little thought, but that there is too much, especially the conscious mind chatter that goes on all day.

There are many predictions about some of the new technology we can expect to see in the future. Although technology will continue to enlarge all of our possibilities for making life easier and more interesting, I do not think it will solve the basic problems of greed and exploitation. For solutions to these problems, I believe we must turn to man's spiritual nature. If man's intuition were to evolve to the point where true intentions are known to all, there would be little opportunity for those of malevolent intent to do harm, and they too would be forced to change.

I believe that the real hope for humanity is not a new invention or scientific discovery, but the development of a true, universal awareness of the connection between all things. As long as we see ourselves as separate, competitive egos in a struggle for survival and a need to dominate, the technology we develop will just serve to strengthen that view, resulting in greater conflicts with even more disastrous outcomes than what has already been experienced.

I did not have to choose between technology and an inner-directed life. However, I did have to find a way of balancing the two, and I continue to strive for that balance today. I am not advocating that we all suddenly become psychic and throw away our computers and mobile phones. The computer, word processing software, web search engines, and mobile phone have certainly made my writing easier, and I don't intend to give them up.

I think that if we all suddenly had access to all of our latent psychic powers, it would be a disaster for man. We would be like children with razor blades, which is an analogy Edgar Cayce once made. However, if these abilities are developed naturally as we are ready for them, then there is the potential for unlimited benefits to humanity.

I found that there is a vast difference between being spiritual and being psychic. Someone can be psychic with little spiritual understanding and misuse their abilities. However, the approach I took and advocate provides a safe way for a person to develop both understanding and intuition under the monitoring of his own better self through meditation and dreams.

I LEARNED THE SIMPLE LESSONS AND TOOK THE SAFE PATH

I noticed the other day when I was out walking that several of the people I passed in the street walked with the traffic. I think we were all taught in elementary school that a person should walk facing traffic in order to see oncoming cars. Some of the people I passed were quite elderly, and many have hearing loss and limited mobility. So they are at risk. And this risk is real because Florida has the unwelcome distinction of having some the worst cities in the United States for pedestrian fatalities.

In February of 2011, while on a walk for Tibet, the Dalai Lama's nephew was hit from behind and killed by a SUV in the evening on a stretch of A1A in Florida. A newspaper article (*Tampa Bay Times*, February 16, 2011) about the accident and his death reported that he wore dark clothing and walked with the flow of traffic instead of against it.

My observation about walkers caused me to reflect on the simple fact that on *the road seldom taken* "I" can see those potential threats coming at me so I know when to stop, move farther to one side, or take some other corrective action. I do not have to be run over by life because I couldn't see what was coming.

Many years ago, I decided to take the road that will show me warnings before tragedies occur and that will provide me with the right turns to make as I traverse the road of life. This road is not mine alone; this road has been known by others who have sought help and guidance in their everyday life through prayer, meditation, and dreams. In this book, I have tried to show how I got on *the road seldom taken* to change the course of my life. My life went from disappointment and misery to fulfillment and a sense of harmony. And with it came a greater understanding of the nature of man and his potential, which forever changed my view of life.

Selected References

Bro, Harmon H. *Edgar Cayce on Dreams*. New York: Paperback Library Edition, 1969.

Cayce, Edgar. *A Search for God, Book I & II*. Association for Research and Enlightenment, 16th edition, 1992.

Clark, Glenn. *The Soul's Sincere Desire*. Kessinger Publishing, 2005.

Climate Change 2013: The Physical Science Basis, www.climat-echange.org.

Hudson, Thomas Jay. *The Law of Psychic Phenomena*. Salinas, CA: Hudson-Cohan Publishing Company, 1977.

Individual Reference File. Edgar Cayce Foundation, 1970.

Krishnamurti, J. *Freedom from the Known*. New York: Harper One, 1975, p. 31.

Robinson, Lynn A. and LaVonne Carlson-Finnerty. *Being Psychic.* Indianapolis: Alpha Books, 1999.

Roberts, Jane. *Seth Speaks.* San Rafael: Amber-Allen Publishing; Novato, CA: New World Library, 1994.

Scallion, Gordon-Michael. *Notes from the Cosmos.* Chesterfield, NH: Matrix Institute, Inc.

Tolle, Eckhart. *The Power of Now.* Novato, CA: New World Library, 1999.

WebMD. *Coping with Excessive Sleepiness, Stages of Sleep: REM and Non-REM Sleep,* http://www.webmd.com/sleep-disorders/excessive-sleepiness-10/sleep-101.

Wilhelm, Richard (translator). *The Secret of the Golden Flower.* San Diego, New York and London: Harcourt Brace Jovanovich Publishers, 1962.

John E. Desautels is a man of dreams—both the metaphorical and the prophetic. He is also a man of action. A Phi Beta Kappa graduate of the University of Vermont with a master's degree in mathematics from The Ohio State University, he spent more than thirty years with the Eastman Kodak Company, serving in managerial positions. He was responsible for the development and implementation of complex software applications and workflow solutions for variable data printing in the Dayton operation.

Desautels was first introduced to the metaphysical concepts of Edgar Cayce prior to launching his career at Kodak. As he began practicing mediation and studying his own dreams, the everyday application of what he learned was as important to him as the philosophy. He learned how to use his dreams as guides to build a better future for himself and the people around him.

Now retired from Kodak, Desautels lives in Largo, Florida, where he writes and continues to study spirituality.

Made in the USA
Las Vegas, NV
09 November 2023

80528950R00077